Secrets of Film Writing

Secrets of Film Writing

Tom Lazarus

ST. MARTIN'S GRIFFIN
NEW YORK

Excerpt from *Stigmata* used with the permission of Metro-Goldwyn-Mayer, Inc.

Excerpt from *Word of Mouth* used with the permission of Playboy Entertainment Group, Inc.

SECRETS OF FILM WRITING. Copyright © 2001 by Tom Lazarus. All rights reserved. Printed in the United States of America. No part of this book may be used or reproduced in any manner whatsoever without written permission except in the case of brief quotations embodied in critical articles or reviews. For information, address St. Martin's Press, 175 Fifth Avenue, New York, N.Y. 10010.

www.stmartins.com

Design by Susan Walsh

Library of Congress Cataloging-in-Publication Data

Lazarus, Tom.
    Secrets of film writing / Tom Lazarus.—1st ed.
        p. cm.
    ISBN 0-312-26908-0
    1. Motion picture authorship.   I. Title.

PN1996.L38 2001
808.2'3—dc21

                                        2001020255

10   9   8   7   6

To my father

CONTENTS

ACKNOWLEDGMENTS

Thank you is inadequate to Ronnie Rubin, who graciously opened the door to teaching for me; to my father, Paul N. Lazarus Jr., who was a role model for me as a teacher and as a man; to Stevie Stern Lazarus, my wife, my student, my teacher; to Alison Lazarus for her support; to Elizabeth Beier for pointing me in the right direction; to Steven Katten for his wisdom; to my brother Paul Lazarus for his read; to Robert Dorian for his impeccable research; to everyone at UCLA Extension for all their support; to my fellow screenwriters who generously allowed me to excerpt their work; to all my students who have put up with my curmudgeonly ways and made me a better teacher; to every producer, development person, network executive and showrunner who has given me notes and helped me become a better writer.

INTRODUCTION

In *The Pat Hobby Stories*, F. Scott Fitzgerald's sad tome about a hack screenwriter in 1930s' Hollywood, Pat Hobby remembers when he and another fellow had fallen on tough times and wrote a book on screenwriting.

They called it *Secrets of Film Writing* and Hobby re ferred to it as "a sucker-trap."

That was the inspiration for writing this book. The title, not the "sucker-trap" part.

I've had a thirty-year career in motion pictures, first creating advertising campaigns, trailers and radio spots for the major studios, then writing on staff for seven television series.

I've written seven produced movies of the week, created five television pilots, written and directed over thirty ed-ucational and business films and documentaries. I've writ-ten close to fifty original feature screenplays, of which six have been made so far.

I've directed three feature films based on my original screenplays and, finally, for the last nine years I've been teaching: Screenwriting, Advanced Screenwriting and

Writing the Feature Film at both UCLA Extension and University of California at Santa Barbara, and a Master Class in Screenwriting for the Graduate School of Radio, Film and Television at California State University Northridge.

Over the years, I've learned some of the secrets of film writing.

Pat Conroy, a helluva writer who wrote *The Great Santini*, *Conrack* and *Prince of Tides* among others, said in the *New York Times* that "writing scripts is simply one of the most difficult things a human being can do."

Knowing that is one of the secrets.

The key for me is that it's "one of the most difficult," but not impossible.

In the pages of this book are the secrets I've learned to write screenplays that are reader friendly, that want to be read, that have to be read.

When a producer or development person, or an actor, or anyone reads one of my scripts, they are not in for an ordeal.

The reading experience is a good one: entertaining, challenging, involving, easy.

The script is usually a page-turner, and even if it isn't what the particular producer's looking for, the read will still be a good one.

If they don't buy this script, maybe they'll give me an assignment or be open to my next pitch.

More than once, I've had a network executive or producer read one of my scripts and call me the next morning. It was right before bed, they told me, they thought they'd pick up the script for a few minutes, then, at two in the morning, they finished it.

Why?

Because I seduced them into reading on, to find out what happens on the next page.

To *have* to know what happens on the next page.

It is the screenwriter's primary job to seduce first the reader, then, ultimately, the viewer.

This reader/viewer is on our side, wanting to be swept away into the evocative world of our making, and they only fall away when we break the implied agreement we have with them. The agreement, a sacred pact, is all about trust. If the reader/viewer agrees to turn him or herself over to the writer and the story they're weaving, we as writers agree not to abuse the trust by not delivering, not respecting, not playing fair on a multitude of levels—all of which I write about later in these pages.

Good screenwriting takes hard work, lots of it, but it's possible.

I'm not sure I agree with Pat Conroy about film writing being "one of the most difficult things a human being can do," but when things aren't going well, I have to admit, his words make me feel better.

I have two goals for *Secrets of Film Writing*. One is to

raise the level of film writing of the writers who read this. And two, through the war stories and discussions of my writing process, to give an insight into what it's like to be a living, breathing and surviving film writer in Hollywood.

There's an ethical and moral dilemma in encouraging screenwriters to raise their writing to another level, and that is: most screenwriters are unemployed, chronically unemployed.

In 1999, only 51.3 percent of the members reporting, or 4,419 writers, of the Writers Guild of America, West actually made money. Of those, only 1,788 made money as feature writers. And in the Writers Guild East, the numbers are even more discouraging.

In Los Angeles, a city of 8 million, where it sometimes seems there are 8 million people writing screenplays, 1,788 money-making writers is scary. At the UCLA Extension Writers Program, where I teach, in the year 2000 there were thirty-five hundred screenwriting students. Three thousand five hundred!?!?!

Tough odds.

A tough road.

I've had close writer friends who've lost their houses, who have had to park their car over the water turnoff so the Department of Water and Power couldn't stop service.

Other writers have gone bankrupt, ended up selling real estate or became Feng Shui experts as they pounded out spec screenplay after spec screenplay, or they just disappeared from Hollywood never to be heard of again.

I've been extremely fortunate to have made a living—sometimes a real good one, sometimes I've been flat broke—doing something I've loved to do. As a get-up-in-the-morning-and-start-work job . . . writing is the best.

What a wonderful way to spend time, solving problems in universes of my own making, playing with characters who respond to my every whim, who don't argue, or complain or do anything that displeases me and, best of all, teach me things.

They say dogs are man's best friend. I don't think so. It's those characters we create, flawed, heroic, human . . . just like us.

I wish you all the joy I get from writing and being a writer . . . and when you sell your screenplay for three million dollars, send me some of the money.

—TOM LAZARUS
www.tomlazarus.com
February 2001

Secrets of Film Writing

Secret #1

Organization Is Freedom

"One of the most basic impulses behind art is the impulse to order the chaos of regular life, to transform it into something more perfect, more shapely and more satisfying, to turn it into something with a beginning, middle and an end."
—Michiko Kakutani

When I was writing an educational film on alcohol dependency, my technical advisor went to great lengths trying to get into my thick skull the concept of Dependency Needs.

It went something like this: we each have dependency needs, things we need. If those dependency needs are met, it frees us not to be dependent. People won't be dependent on alcohol if their dependency needs are met, particularly early in life.

Okay, I apply that to screenwriting. **If my Organization Needs are met, it frees me to write creatively.**

What does that actually mean?

How do we organize stories?

Beginning, middle and end is an organization. The details and textures of the story interweave around and through the beginning, middle and end.

Writers use outlines, or beat sheets, or treatments, or information on index cards, among other systems. All of these are **Story Organizers**.

If you satisfy your organization needs of structure and flow by one of the above devices, then, if my theory holds, you can write freely and creatively because if you stick close enough to the spine of your story, as plotted through your scene list, you'll always be moving the story forward.

The **Scene List** is my Story Organizer.

Here's what it looks like for a script called *Dead Serious*.

Simon Sweeney ordering up a screenwriter.

Arthur Pratt, the writer, meeting with Sweeney.

Arthur thrown out of Sweeney's office at studio.

Arthur at bar with Graff, who was a film writer and now makes living as a bartender and garbageman.

Arthur dumped by girlfriend, who becomes an agent.

Arthur comes up with the million-dollar idea.

Arthur tries to get to Sweeney. Fails.

Arthur breaks into Sweeney's house. Busted.

Chase.

Arthur makes his stand on the Hollywood sign.

Arthur becomes folk hero.

Sweeney buys his screenplay.

Arthur on top of the world.

Sweeney's out at the studio.

The deal for the screenplay doesn't happen.

Arthur is sued by studio and pilloried by the studio spin machine.

Arthur tries to get work in TV and is shunned due to age.

Arthur tracks down Sweeney, now a potato farmer, to resurrect project and themselves.

Sweeney sets the dogs on him.

Arthur's agent drops him.

Arthur looks around and realizes he's nowhere.

Arthur goes to Hollywood sign to commit suicide, and is discovered again.

Arthur on way to becoming media darling redux.

The scene list is a concise, conceptual way to see the structure and flow of the whole piece.

When I started writing, I would **color and shape code** the scene list:

A dot next to action scenes.

A box next to talk scenes.

A circle for the main character.

A triangle for the antagonist.

A diamond for the woman lead.

With a sweep of my eye down the single-spaced scene list, I could get the rhythm of the piece, how the action scenes were separated, how far apart similar scenes were. I could spot when I'd let a B or C story die and where I could insert something to keep that part of the story alive.

And it's only a list of scenes. It's not prose. You don't have to spend time "writing" the damn thing.

The scene list is a tool.

4

When you're at the beginning stages of your scene list, **don't censor** any scenes, put them all down, **let your story tell itself.**

Don't try to fit it into some preconceived form or structure, meaning trying to torture your story into someone else's generic, low-common-denominator structure that may not be at all relevant to the story you're telling.

Every story has its own integrity.

Let the story logically tell itself. There isn't just one "right" logic for a story. Your logic is your logic. It's right. Trust it and not someone who says certain parts of your story should happen on specific pages.

Take chances in the early stages of conceptualizing your story.

Don't do it the way you've seen other movies made, or stories told.

Go for it, because no one's going to see it.

It's a process.

There is no wrong way.

Put it down, then read it and re-logic it.

Don't show it to anyone.

Try it different ways. Be open. Listen to yourself. Become sensitive to what you feel as well as think about the story. The scene list, at this point, isn't what you want your script to be, but it's a beginning, the vital first step in the process of getting the screenplay out of your head and down on a sheet of paper, the first step in an exciting journey.

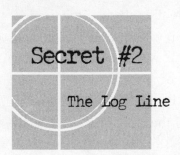

Secret #2

The Log Line

The best log line I've ever read was for an episode of the old TV show *Father Knows Best*. It was: Billy loses his house key. That's what the episode was about. That, and nothing more.

The log line is the simple, one- or two-sentence, description of a movie that appears in *TV Guide*.

The log line is another invaluable tool in writing your screenplay.

Log lines are vital in my process of film writing because they force me to distill my idea for the screenplay down to its essence.

The log line is what I judge what I'm writing against.

The log line forces me to be absolutely clear about what I'm writing.

To the neverending chagrin of my much-beleaguered

students, I force them, as a first step in the screenwriting process, to discipline their minds and come up with their log lines.

It compels them to think about the basics of their idea.

When a writer can't come up with a simple distillation of their idea, then their idea may not be clear in their minds or the idea itself might be flawed.

I had one student, Louis, who I felt was really writing three different screenplays: (1) the story of a girl; (2) the story of the girl's lover; (3) the story of the girl's mother. Louis designed the stories so they intersected at the end of the screenplay.

The problem was Louis couldn't come up with a simple, coherent log line. It kept getting convoluted and confused. I sensed he was trying to tell too many stories and told him so.

But Louis stuck to his guns. He said that was the screenplay he wanted to write. I thought he was wrong, but those are the breaks.

After about fifty pages of writing on the script, Louis announced he was splitting the screenplay into two separate scripts . . . he couldn't make it work as one. And then, when I asked him the log lines for the two different scripts, he had them . . . and they were clear and concise.

If the story you're writing isn't clear, then your writing won't be clear either.

The log line for *Dead Serious* is:

Screenwriter Arthur's hilarious descent into Hollywood oblivion and back again.

That means everything I write is judged against this log line to see if I'm writing the screenplay I want to be writing.

There is a tendency to drift, to get lost. The log line keeps you honest.

The log line keeps us close to **the spine or center line of the story** . . . we need every tool we can get.

Notice please that **the main character** is at the center of my log line.

This is vital (see Secret # 3: TELLING THE STORY THROUGH THE CHARACTERS).

Another way to evaluate the script you're going to be writing is to imagine what the trailer and ad campaign would be. How would a studio sell your movie? It will give you insights as to what you should concentrate on and emphasize in your writing.

A way to think about what you're writing is to imagine yourself meeting with the head of the studio and having to explain why, among the myriad other projects they're considering, he or she should make a deal for your script.

In the case of the script in this book, *Dead Serious*, the commercial elements, or **reasons to make it**, include:

> **A tour de force main character** which can attract
> an actor, a real plus for any project.

A hilarious story about Hollywood. Even though the conventional wisdom in this town is a script about Hollywood will never get made . . . yet, take a look, they—the studios, independents, cable, everyone—are always making movies about movies. It's a stealth genre.

A memorable set piece action scene of Arthur holding off the SWAT unit from the Hollywood sign. It's the ad campaign, the trailer, what people remember.

A modest budget.

I'm the nephew of the head of the studio.

The last reason points up one of the great intangibles about Hollywood. **Deals are made for many reasons, both good and bad.**

An example: I was visiting a friend of mine, let's call him Sid, who was president of Global Marketing for a major studio. Before lunch with him one day, I went with him to a screening of a rough cut of a trailer, the short "coming attractions" piece that runs in theaters prior to a film showing. It was an okay trailer of an obviously expensive period piece about a composer's life. After the lights went up and Sid gave his input to Josh, the bootlicking head of the trailer department (not really, but I couldn't resist the image), he turned to me and asked me what I thought. I said the trailer was fine, but more importantly, I asked him why in God's name had the studio made this movie which, at least to me, seemed destined for the video stores the morning it opened. Sid shrugged a world-weary shrug and said the studio wanted to be "in bed" with the producers so they made this vanity film which was one of the producers' pet projects. Thus, the picture was made.

Another example: I was asked by the Leonard Goldberg Company to work with them developing a pilot for a TV series for ABC. I did meetings with a wonderful development executive named Deborah Aal, who used to have the largest collection of cashmere sweaters in Hollywood, and we came up with a terrific pitch for an hour-long project called *Three Men and a Boat*.

Leonard Goldberg, a former president of ABC, a very plugged-in Hollywood player, my newest best friend, accompanied us into the pitch.

There was, of course, the prerequisite schmoozing, then I went into my pitch. After six minutes of perspiration-soaked hell, I finished. There was a beat, then the ABC development exec said, "Yes." "Yes?" I stammered. She nodded yes. I was given a go into script on the spot. Unheard of.

Why did this happen?

Not because of the genius of my pitch. Not because of the brilliance of the project or how good a person I am, or how shiny my shoes were. Not because of anything other than sitting next to me was the 800-pound gorilla named Leonard Goldberg. I think if I had pitched the hip-hop version of the Koran she would have said yes.

I know projects that have been given the go-ahead because the pitcher/writer had large breasts, good drugs, was a friend of a friend, you get the idea.

The only other time I was given a go in the room was at NBC on a project I created called *Breaking Story*, the behind-the-scenes drama at a CNN-like cable news network during a coup d'etat in Washington. They said "go" in the room because the 800-pound gorilla was my partner on the project and my newest best friend, feature director Joe Dante, the man who has given the world *Gremlins* and *Small Soldiers*, among others. A feature director crossing over into TV . . . worthy of a "yes" in the room.

Breaking Story, by the way, like most projects, never saw the light of day. After writing two full drafts, I was replaced on my own project by a late-arriving, dim-witted network executive. She didn't feel I was "right for the project" I created. Excuse me?

But, I digress.

Secret #3

Telling the Story Through the Characters

At the center of every story are the characters. They are who we, as the readers/viewers, identify with.

We experience the story through the characters and your job as the writer is to **put them in the center of your script**.

Actors get movies made.

If you don't have a castable part, a part that an actor is dying to play, it will be harder, if not impossible, to get that script made.

The bigger and more challenging a role, the better and more bankable an actor will be attracted to it, and the better chance you have of getting your screenplay seriously considered.

I don't know if it's true, but an agent, a notoriously untrustworthy bunch if you ask me, told me of the Jane Fonda Rule.

He swore to me that Jane Fonda, when she received a script from her agents, leafed quickly through the script and, unless she found at least three page-long monologues where her character talked from the heart, she threw the script in the garbage.

Apocryphal or not, the Jane Fonda Rule is real on some level. I know actors who only read their lines in the script. Those same actors count their lines.

One of the times my career was in the toilet, I purposely set out to write a scenery-chewing, tour de force performance for the main character for the reasons outlined above. I wrote the script *Weird City*, the log line of which is: a detective fakes manic depression and goes undercover into group therapy to find the killer of two psychiatrists.

This is how that script opened:

WEIRD CITY
Written by Tom Lazarus

FADE IN:

INT. DR. STRASSER'S OFFICE - DAY
(PATIENT'S POV)

DR. STRASSER, graying beard, tweed jacket, bow tie and running shoes, sits in a well-worn, comfortable chair, legs crossed, toying with a fat black Mont Blanc ball point pen.

> DR. STRASSER
> (into CAMERA)

I think, frankly, we have a lot of work ahead of us. The different aspects of your personality aren't . . . aren't integrated and that lack of integration is causing you anxiety and stress, particularly . . .
> (carefully)

. . . in your relationships with the opposite sex.
> (quickly)

Now, don't get excited, please. I know that upsets you, but I don't want you to say anything. Just think about all this, digest it, and we'll deal with it in group or in our session next week.

Dr. Strasser stands.

> DR. STRASSER
> (continuing; supportive)

We have to talk about all this, it's the only way you're going to really understand and get by it . . . and I'm confident you will.
> (smiling)

See you next week.

INT. PARKING STRUCTURE - THAT
NIGHT - (PATIENT'S POV)

The elevator opening in the distance. Talking
on a cellular phone, Dr. Strasser, exits the elevator and heads toward the Range Rover parked
against the wall in the nearly empty parking
structure.

> DR. STRASSER
> Need anything at the store?
>> (listening, then)
> Okay, I'll see you in half an hour.

He switches off the phone, puts it in his pocket,
then heads for the car. As he walks up to the
Range Rover, he turns off the car alarm with a
HIGH-PITCHED BEEP BEEP. CAMERA
MOVES QUICKLY toward him. Hearing
RUSHING FEET, Dr. Strasser starts to turn
when a black nylon rope slips around his neck
choking him.

> DR. STRASSER
> (continuing)
> ARRRRRRGGGGHHHHHHH!

Dr. Strasser's hands reach back over his head
trying to get to the unseen strangler's gloved

hands, but it's useless. After a few moments, he's thrown back against the car, GASPING HORRIBLY for air through his injured windpipe. Dr. Strasser's eyes look right into CAMERA and widen in absolute horror. BANG! A bullet tears into Dr. Strasser's chest SLAMMING him back against the Range Rover. BANG! Another bullet pumps into Dr. Strasser, who looks down in stunned disbelief at the growing stains of blood on his shirt. BANG! BANG! Two more bullets THUMP into Dr. Strasser, causing him to slide awkwardly down to the cement floor. As he lies sprawled on his back, eyes staring straight ahead, BANG! BANG! Two more bullets slam into his already lifeless body. THUMPA THUMPA THUMPA. BLACK SCREEN - TITLES The THUMPA THUMPA THUMPA THROB of a helicopter. Red MAIN TITLES over evocative black and white ink blots.

POLICE DISPATCHER'S VOICE
(garbled)
Bird Three . . . STATIC . . . we've got a 415
. . . STATIC. What is your position?

INT. POLICE HELICOPTER - NIGHT

The glowing red and green displays of the complex cockpit dash. The PILOT switches on his

17

radio and fights to talk over the THUMPA
THUMPA of the blades rotating above him.

> PILOT
> (on radio)
> Copy, One. We're above the Ten, spinning
> South.

EXT. SANTA MONICA - NIGHT

DEAN MCPHEE, mid-thirties, eyes wild, veins
on his neck bulging, sweat pouring off him, is
absolutely crazed as he stalks around the lawn in
front of the modest clapboard bungalow, YELL-
ING at the top of his lungs.

> MCPHEE
> Get your flabby ass on out here you no
> good fuckin' scumbucket!

There are lights on in the house, but no re-
sponse.

> MCPHEE
> (continuing)
> You don't think I know there's some dick-
> head in there? You don't think I know it? I
> know it!! I FUCKIN' KNOW IT!!!

AN ELDERLY WOMAN NEIGHBOR in a
bathrobe peeks warily through the hedge between houses.

                    MCPHEE
            (continuing; to the neighbor)
      Get back in there!

Instantly, the neighbor disappears behind the
hedge.

EXT. SANTA MONICA SKY - HELICOPTER
POV - NIGHT

The lights of Los Angeles spread East from the
ocean.

            POLICE DISPATCHER'S VOICE
      STATIC . . . location . . . STATIC . . . Shell
      and Kenwood. Black and white's on its
      way.

INT. POLICE HELICOPTER - NIGHT

The lights of L.A. reflect in the pilot's visor.

                    PILOT
                (into radio)
      Copy One.

He banks radically to the West.

EXT. SANTA MONICA BUNGALOW - NIGHT

McPhee stops at the front walk. He's frantic.

                    MCPHEE
          Okay, motherfucker, it's mano a mano
          time.

He reaches behind him into his waist holster,
pulls out an efficient-looking silver and black
9mm Glock and lays it on the grass.

                    MCPHEE
                    (continuing)
          No more gun.
                    (tearing off his Hawaiian shirt)
          No more shirt. No more bullshit. Hey, I'm
          just some freak. You can take me. Come
          on, sucker, you don't get my woman with-
          out having to come through me first!

EXT. VENICE - NIGHT (AERIAL SHOT)

The Police helicopter cruises low over the roof-
tops of Venice.

INT. POLICE HELICOPTER - NIGHT

The OFFICER in the passenger seat unsnaps his holster and slides the safety off on his Smith and Wesson. The Pilot looks out the bubble window.

                    PILOT
        This is Bird Three. Looks like we're here.

He flicks his <u>BEAM</u> switch.

EXT. HELICOPTER - NIGHT

Hanging from the nose, the huge Halogen light CRACKS ON.

EXT. SANTA MONICA BUNGALOW - NIGHT

THUMPA THUMPA THUMPA. Bathed in the bright Police searchlight, McPhee doesn't seem to notice the helicopter.

                    MCPHEE
                  (shouting)
        You got a minute, Harelip, sixty seconds,
        then I come in there drag your sorry ass out.

Over McPhee's shoulder, a black and white Police unit, its lights spinning red, pulls to a stop at the curb.

MCPHEE
(continuing; to shout)
Okay, Hemorrhoid, read 'em and fuckin'
weep! You got thirty seconds!!

The doors of the black and white open. Holstering their batons, two OFFICERS climb out and warily head for McPhee.

MCPHEE
(continuing)
All right, man, I'm going to do it your
fuckin' way.

OFFICER
Excuse me, sir.

McPhee turns and sees the two Officers approaching cautiously.

OFFICER TWO
What's the problem here?

MCPHEE
No problem.
(then turning back to the house, "playfully")
Ready or not, here I come!

The Officers move between McPhee and the house.

OFFICER

Forget it, Pal, you're not going anywhere.
What's the deal? What's going on?

Behind the officers, the front door opens and
CARRIE, late twenties, barefoot, beautiful in
shorts and a singlet, moves out onto the porch.
She's been crying.

CARRIE

Just get him out of here, okay? He's out of
his mind.

McPhee turns toward her.

MCPHEE
(sarcastically)
Thank you, Doctor.
(to the cops)
I'm the sane one around here.
(shaking his head at Carrie)
Look at the way you're dressed . . . why
don't you come the hell out here fuckin'
naked?

He looks over her shoulder.

MCPHEE
(continuing)
Where's Long Dong Silver?

CARRIE

There's no one here!

Officer Two moves toward the house as the
other Officer stands in front of McPhee.

OFFICER

Now, I'm going to want you to walk over
to my vehicle and put your hands on the
trunk . . . and I don't want any trouble.

McPhee stares at him with those intensely crazy
eyes. The Officer doesn't like that look at all
and unholsters his Smith and Wesson.

OFFICER
(continuing)
Okay, get over by the unit! Now!

McPhee looks at him for another long moment,
then slowly raises his hands over his head and
walks toward the black and white. Carrie sits on
the front steps crying.

CARRIE
(to Officer Two)
It's insanity, it really is. We broke up last
week and he went nuts.

OFFICER
(indicating the house)
If you've got a guy in there, you . . .

CARRIE
(interrupting, frustrated)
There's no one in there!

OFFICER
Did he hit you?

Carrie shakes her head.

CARRIE
He put his gun down over there.

OFFICER
Gun?!?!

Carrie points to the Glock in the grass. Officer
Two heads for the gun.

OFFICER TWO
(over his shoulder)
You going to want to press charges here?

Carrie hesitates a moment, then closes her eyes
and shakes her head sadly. McPhee's up against
the car, hands on the trunk and legs spread, as
the Officer pulls his pants pockets inside out

searching for weapons or contraband. Officer
Two approaches with McPhee's gun at the same
time the Officer pulls a Santa Monica Police
Detective's shield out of McPhee's back pocket.
The two Officers look at each other in disbelief.

A mercurial character right from FADE IN:, McPhee is
an over-the-top turn and received a great deal of praise
from everyone who read the script.

Weird City was optioned by MCA and the USA channel within two weeks of it being sent out by my agent. I
was told by the talented and nice production executive
Barbara Fisher at MCA that they felt the script "would
attract a major piece of talent."

The script was never made. Why? Well, the best I was
able to glean from the funereal silence that follows a network pass, when no one will return your phone call, or
think of calling you with an update . . . pass . . . everything's always great until they pass.

I was told it was a pass because the powers that be at
USA felt the sex in the script was too kinky. The endless
violent murders weren't any problem, but the two safe-
sex, out of frame masturbation scenes were too much for
them. And I couldn't even rewrite it. The executive at
USA was terminally turned off.

There's a lesson to be learned here, I just have no idea
what it is.

Secret #4

Rising Action

The classic three-act structure:

Act 1 pages 1–30

Act 2 pages 31–85

Act 3 pages 86–110

is a good reference, good for talking about and analyzing screenplays, but, in my admittedly controversial opinion, is horribly outdated as a structure for motion picture scripts. Here's where purists slam this book closed and fling it out the window.

Quickly, let me explain:

• In these media-pervasive times we live in, the number

of stories we're exposed to is endless. We see round the clock story after story in movies and television, commercials, a seamless ribbon of storytelling, beginnings, middles and ends. We've all become so story hip, the classical structure is no longer as useful as it once was.

The three-act structure in movies has been to use the first act to set up the characters, lay the pipe of the story, set up and establish things until the end of the act where "the story," or log line, kicks in.

Very nice. It works. There's nothing wrong with it . . . but, in this world of nanoseconds, it's too slow, way too slow. We're totally used to remote controlling our way out of stories when we're the slightest bit bored.

Even when we're in the movie theater, our mind is remote controlling us, trying to get the story going faster, looking to get out the moment things become boring.

We're smart readers and viewers. The powers that be don't believe it, but I do.

We know if we introduce Arthur Pratt in *Dead Serious* being thrown out of studio head Simon Sweeney's office, what's going to be happening here. It's a bad thing when the reader is ahead of the writer.

If all the above is true, what replaces the three-act structure?

Rising Action.

If you learn only one thing from this book, let it be about rising action.

An example of rising action: if you're writing a movie

about a serial killer, in the first ten pages your killer stabs a man to death.

The next killing has to be more gruesome. Let's say he hacks a man to death with a razor-sharp machete.

Fine.

The next murder has to be even more. More graphic. More horrible. More something. The key here, obviously, is more.

You have to keep delivering more, every step of the way.

Let's say you're writing a romance. The love scenes in the first ten pages are tame. Then, the next time, passionate. The third sex scene is unbridled desire. The fourth: lust. Five: uncontrolled passion.

If it's a war story, it starts with a skirmish, evolves into a clash, then a fight, then a battle; finally, at the end of act three, a war.

And so on. Like that.

Rising action.

A vital concept to making your script a page turner.

I've used the term page turner. What do I mean? It's a script where you've put out enough interesting character and story to grab the reader, but you are, at the same time, withholding enough additional information to keep them tuned in, having to find out what's going to happen.

It's this **disclose/hold back tension,** always giving the reader/viewer payoffs along the way, but at the same time, promising ever more satisfying payoffs down the road.

If it's true that our minds want to find order in the chaos, what delicious tension is set up by disclosure/hold back of an evolving, rising story.

Our job as screenwriters is to seduce the reader, to make them want to, <u>have</u> to, turn the pages to see what happens next.

If they read your script and know what's going to happen, know what the structure is in advance, what fun is that?

Readers, executives, agents, assistants, go home for the weekend with a stack of scripts to do coverage on.

If they're not turned on by your script, and turned on fast, they will inevitably put it down.

Bad.

If they don't know what's coming. If you're true to your story and it doesn't fit into an already hackneyed structure, the action rises and the main character is in the center of the piece, you're way ahead.

Good.

Real good.

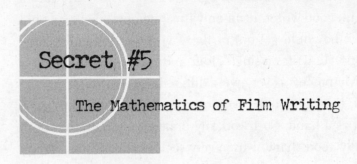

Secret #5

The Mathematics of Film Writing

The more you write the better it gets.

It's that simple.

Good night.

I know a writer, let's call him Herm, and he's written with me on a number of TV shows. His office is always the most interestingly decorated: personal memorabilia and totems, pyramids, a portrait of the Dalai Lama, walls filled with friendly images, Herm on horseback, on the set, with his actress wife. While he was fussing with his office for the first two weeks we were employed, I was banging out an episode.

Herm procrastinates. He'll do anything but write. His wife calls half a dozen times a day, it's car trouble, the dentist, the chiropractor, an alien sighting, testifying in a lawsuit, anything but writing until the deadline is upon him; then, and only then, under the gun, can he write. And he's a damn good writer. I can only imagine how good he would be if he could get out of the way of himself and do the work. He writes a single draft and he's finished.

My process is very, very different.

I, like many other writers, am just waiting to be found out as a fraud. So I work my brains out to get a script in really good shape. I use every second allotted me. When I was younger and impossibly stupid and needy, so eager to please, I would start writing before the deal closed. I was only burned once, when the producer said the deal was a "slam dunk," only it wasn't. These days, I wait.

I really try and start by conceptualizing the film as a whole, so after figuring out **my log line**, I get yellow pads out so I can make notes of everything; scenes, character ideas, names, thoughts, themes, research, anything that comes to mind, with no censoring, writing everything down.

Then, when I can't wait any longer and I have to start finding order in the chaos, **I do my first scene list.** I work on that a while, expanding it, changing it, trying things, taking chances, then when I can't *not* write script pages, when I have to start, I embark on my **rough draft** and type FADE IN:.

I write like a banshee, thirty, maybe forty pages—the joy of writing—basically the first act, all energy, all enthusiasm, fast out of the blocks. It usually takes me two days, then I stop, come up for air and **read** what I've done.

Then, I do a cursory rewrite of those pages, redo the first part of the scene list based on what I've written, then redo the second third of the scene list to reflect the evolving story and start writing script pages again.

Because writing is a continually creative process, things change as you write, new twists and turns and permutations occur to you. You have to keep updating your scene list to reflect that.

I stop at about page seventy-five or eighty, take another deep breath, read and rewrite, redo the scene list for the second part, redo the unwritten part of the scene list, crank up and start writing again. I write until I get to FADE OUT:.

I celebrate, jump up and down, and think I'm terrific. Then, I settle down and get ready to rewrite.

I'll do about six or seven passes, that's right, **six or seven full, write every wrong, passes,** then finally I've got my rough draft.

At this point, I'll get some input on it from readers and start rewriting.

The rule is: **The more you write, the better your script will get.**

Secret #6

Less Is More

"Art is the elimination of the unnecessary."
—Pablo Picasso

EXT. BEVERLY HILLS MANSION - SUNSET
A pearlescent champagne-colored 2001 Jaguar
convertible, its tires slick with Armorall, sweeps up
the herringbone bricked driveway to the dark
wood and beige stucco faux Tudor mansion three
blocks North of Sunset. The sun glares in the
crystal-clean driver's side window as SIMON
SWEENEY, 35, a handsome, Armani-clad mogul
of the first order, tearing his maroon and yellow
paisley power tie from around the neck of his blue
and white striped J. Press shirt, climbs out, places
the expensive door closed rather than slamming

it, and rushes up the rough-hewn granite steps to
the massive carved oak front door. He opens the
unlocked door and enters, SLAMMING the
huge door closed behind him.

Too much detail.
Way, way too much detail.
The deal is: **write this amount of detail only in the
important scenes,** only when it's story relevant, only when
you damn well have a good reason.

Simon Sweeney driving up to his house and entering
is a transition scene at best. Who knows if it'll appear in
the final cut or even the final draft of the script. If you
write that amount of detail throughout your script, the
reader won't be able to discern what is important. I've
read scripts where everything is described and written in
excruciating detail.

It's tiring and boring and ultimately terminal.

What that transition scene should read like:

EXT. BEVERLY HILLS MANSION - SUNSET
Simon Sweeney's Jaguar pulls up to the front
door. Pulling his tie off, Simon gets out and
rushes into the house.

You, as the writer, have to take responsibility to guide the
reader as to what's important simply by the way you write
it. I call it **"weighting"** a script.

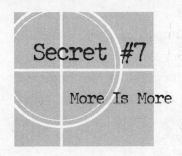

Secret #7

More Is More

"All you need is four good scenes."
— Frank Capra

Different parts of the script should be written in different ways.

The complement to less is more.

The gold scenes:

the big set piece action scenes,

the important, pivotal scenes,

the scenes that will appear in the trailer,

the scenes where your characters reveal the essential truths about themselves, should be written fully and completely, weighted heavy. More is more.

The transition scenes, the unimportant ones, should be written minimally. Less is more.

The not-so-gold scenes: cut them out of your script and wrap fish with them or rewrite them to make them good.

Secret #8

Script Presentation

Anything but perfect, studio acceptable format lessens your chances for success.

If a reader sees your incorrectly formatted script, they consciously or unconsciously don't like it.

That's bad news.

The good news: perfect format is easily within your grasp.

Use any one of the popular screenwriting programs. I use Scriptware, but Final Draft, Movie Master, and Script Thing are all reasonably good and they will all format your script consistently and correctly.

If you want to see how screenplays should look and have no access to typed screenplays in their original form, go on the Internet and you can find them there.

Some other thoughts on the presentation of your script:

Don't suggest casting, but take responsibility and describe your characters so the reader has a visual to hold on to and relate to.

Don't include a synopsis or character biographies. It encourages producers and readers not to read. And if there's anything in the world they don't need, it's encouragement not to read.

How long should your screenplay be? Not less than 95 pages or more than 125.

I've written screenplays as long as 135 pages. That's okay, if there's a reason for it. Most movies are ninety-something minutes and some are as long as three hours.

The industry standard is that **each page is a minute.** That's how it averages out.

For a while, I was having screenplays come in at 117 pages. I don't have screenplays less than 105 unless I'm directing a low-budget feature. When I shot *Movies Kill*— a feature that's still sitting on the shelf due to the incipient craziness of my producer, who won't let me finish the picture, but that's another story—I shot a ninety-three-page script.

Each page represented a minute and the schedule was so tight—I was shooting twelve pages a day—I pared the script down to the bare bones.

What about cheating? Your script is too long so you widen the margins. Cool. You make the dialogue blocks wider. Yeah, that's it. You program longer pages, use a smaller font. That's the ticket. Your script is short, you shrink the margins, shorten the pages, enlarge the font . . .

Forget it.

You're fooling no one.

There are a few different standard studio formats. Whichever format you pick, be consistent and stick with it.

Some writers use CUT TO: after every scene. I don't, as you've seen in the script samples in this book. I double space so there's a visual space, something that cues the eye there's a new scene, without the incredibly redundant and obvious CUT TO:.

Don't put in scene numbers until you are readying your script for production that is, after you've sold it, bought a new Mercedes and become insufferable.

Before that, numbers are truly excess baggage and excess baggage gets in the way of the seduction of the reader.

How do you bind your script? Again, use the studio standard: brads and those little disc things that flatten the ends of the brads. Good binding is a courtesy to your readers. That's the business you're in.

Respect your readers. My father, to whom *Secrets of Film Writing* is dedicated, was in the motion picture business all his life, mostly in advertising, with a little producing. Then, after he retired, he taught screenwriting at University of California at Santa Barbara for seventeen years, where he rightfully became an institution and where there's a screenwriting scholarship in his and my mother's names. He challenged students in each class to have perfect scripts and promised each one of them a dollar at the end of the semester if they didn't make any of the following mistakes:

Misuse of **they're** or **their** or **there**

Misuse of **it's** or **its**

Misuse of **your** or **you're**

Misuse of **are** or **our**

Misuse of **lets** or **let's**

Misuse of **to, two, too**

Misuse of **who's, whose**

Misuse of **lay** or **lie**

To my knowledge, he never paid anyone a single dollar.

What does this mean to you're script!
Every time a reader reads you're script, their bounced out of it because its you're mistakes that our doing it. Lets make a pack and get are format perfect,

An example of perfect format:

DEAD SERIOUS
Written by Tom Lazarus

FADE IN:

EXT. BIG PICTURE STUDIOS - DAY
The heat waves distort the soundsta-
ges and backlot making it look like
they're reflected in a fun house mirror. It's appropriate.

EXT. EXECUTIVE ROW - DAY
The bright sun glinting off the
pristine Mercedes and Jaguars
parked in front of the two-story
Spanish-style studio building

INT. SWEENEY'S OFFICE - DAY
A sign on the desk: <u>The Duck Stops
Here</u>. Wearing a headset phone, his
expensive jacket perfect on the back
of his leather desk chair, SIMON
SWEENEY paces around his sun-
drenched office.

                    SWEENEY
I need someone who can rewrite
without any of that bullshit
writer crap.

                  AGENT'S VOICE
                (over the phone)
I got the guy. He's a real pro. A
writer's writer.

                    SWEENEY
I don't want one of those brilliant ones, you know what I'm
saying?

                  AGENT'S VOICE
                (over the phone)
I got the perfect guy: Arthur
Pratt, guaranteed not bril-
liant.

EXT. SWEENEY'S OUTER OFFICE –
THE NEXT DAY

On the door to the private office:
SIMON SWEENEY, GLOBAL PRESIDENT OF
PRODUCTION.

ARTHUR PRATT, late forties, a once
handsome man now with hair a bit too

thin, stomach hanging a bit too much
over his worn leather belt, and the
desperation a little bit too appar-
ent in his sad eyes.

                    SWEENEY'S VOICE
                         (O.S.)
          I hate this! It's shit, pure
          shit! This jerk couldn't write
          his way out of a paper asshole.

In slacks and a silk shirt, Arthur
wipes the perspiration off his fore-
head as TIFFANY, 23, Sweeney's pneu-
matic blonde assistant, answers the
phone and looks at him as if he were
a production assistant.

                    TIFFANY
                    (into the phone)
          Put Mr. Katten on.
                    (beat, insistent)
          Put Mr. Katten on first.
                    (pause, victorious)
          Thank you. He'll be right with
          you.

She presses the intercom.

                    TIFFANY
                (continuing)
        I have your call.

        She hangs up the phone and turns to
        the perspiring Arthur.

                    TIFFANY
                (continuing)
            Yes?

                    ARTHUR
        Arthur Pratt.

        Tiffany smiles now that she knows
        who he is.

                    TIFFANY
        I'm Tiffany, Mr. Sweeney's
        Executive Assistant.

        Arthur holds out his hand to shake.
        Tiffany's reluctant to touch the
        writer but finally shakes.

                    TIFFANY
                (continuing)
        Mr. Sweeney will be with you in
        just a minute. Can I get you some
        water or coffee?

                    ARTHUR
        I'll have a decaf soy latte.

    Tiffany looks at him with a pained
    smile and presses the phone button.

                    TIFFANY
               (into the phone)
         Mr. Sweeney's office.

    Arthur's about to explain, but
    doesn't. He looks around, then moves
    to the leather couch and making Tif-
    fany ook up in disgust. Arthur sags.
    It's going to be a long day.

The **format rules** here are:

Begin every script with FADE IN:

Every slug line:
EXT. SWEENEY'S OFFICE-DAY

has to be followed by stage direction:
Beads of sweat drip down Arthur
Pratt's face as Sweeney looks over
his pages.

Many inexperienced writers leave out the stage direction.

When you introduce a speaking character CAPI-TALIZE THE NAME. Don't capitalize the name after that.

Double-space between scenes to get a visual cut which replaces the antiquated CUT TO:.

Only put on the page what is necessary.

CUT TO: is not needed.

Nor is CONTINUED on the top and bottom of each page. Save those details for the production draft . . . that's when they are needed. Putting them in will raise your page count by a few pages.

Always include INT. or EXT. and DAY or NIGHT on every slug line, which is the line that gives the technical information of each scene.

Ultimately, when your script is bought and while you're in Paris celebrating, the film goes into pre-production, and the script is boarded. Each scene is broken out of your script and put on a production board. They're put there according to their sequence of production. EXT. and INT. scenes are put together. DAY and NIGHT scenes as well. It is important that the slug line carries all the necessary information.

Whenever something is read on screen: a sign-
The Duck Stops Here, a note, a marquee, titles,
the time, skywriting, it is _underlined_.

All sounds, like PFFFFFFFFFT, are CAPITAL-
IZED.

When a character speaks in two dialogue blocks in
a row, the second dialogue block has to have (**continued**) below the character name.

When using (**Off Screen**) the first time, use the
full words. After that you can use (**O.S.**).

The same is true with (**Voice Over**), which later
becomes (**V.O.**).

Secret #9

Show Not Tell

"A picture is worth a thousand words."
—Old Chinese Saying

Movies are a visual medium.

It is your job as the film writer to **constantly reinforce the visuals** so the reader can always, yes, always, **see** what is going on.

Look at **the design of your pages.**

If there are only dialogue blocks with no descriptions or stage directions, you're writing radio.

And if you think it's tough making a living writing for film, try radio.

When rewriting, take a draft and try to eliminate all the dialogue that can be replaced by a character's gesture or action.

Check through a draft to see if any of your characters are **telling** us something that would better serve your story by **seeing** it.

Try and see the movie and where there are potential opportunities to describe an important visual better, where description of action or tone and mood would make a scene work better.

What about lighting?

How do you describe light in your script?

How does the way you describe the light affect the mood of the scene?

When rewriting, go through a draft and see what dialogue you can outright take out.

Writers depend too much on telling readers things in screenplays and not nearly enough on describing telling human behavior.

Secret #10

Write Short

Try to **write an eighty to eighty-five page rough draft.**
Why?

Early in my career, I was writing impossibly long rough drafts, sometimes as long as 160 pages.

I was being free, being creative . . . being undisciplined.

Then came the impossible task of trying to squeeze 160 pages down into 110–120 pages. I had to cut scenes I loved, shorten things, shortcut the logic and I was an unhappy writer.

Now, when I write short rough drafts, I can add to the script where I want to. In the important scenes, I have the freedom to expand them, to add nuances, gold and weight to the script.

The script I'm writing during one of the drafts of this book is called *K'ang Mi*. It's about a woman's discovery of the abominable snowman.

My first rough draft came out at eighty-eight pages.

I rewrote it to ninety-six pages and gave it to someone to read. Based on those notes and my thoughts, I rewrote it to 107 pages.

I want to add five more pages of big character scenes with my main characters and I should be there. Without cutting anything I didn't want to.

The next rewrite of *K'ang Mi* came in at 110 pages, after having pulled out nine of the first twenty-three, then adding more gold scenes with the heartwarming K'ang Mi.

These changes came at a prospective agent's suggestion. I gave her that and my other scripts, *In the Belly of the Beast* and 3, to read as samples for possible representation.

She gave me notes on *K'ang Mi* and didn't mention representation.

After more rewriting and notes from two trusted readers, I expanded the script to 123 pages. It's richer, fuller and I really like it. I think it's the most commercial script I've written to date.

Probably the kiss of death.

Ultimately, the agency agreed to represent me. They work hard on my behalf and are terrifically nice. To this date, they haven't gotten me any work. They get my name out, circulate my work, introduce me to people, lots of support which I don't take lightly at all, but no work.

DISSOLVE TO:

INT. LAZARUS MANSION - DAY
His trusty hounds Morgan and Ruby at his feet,
TOM, the author, polishes his manuscript
Secrets of Film Writing.

TOM
(into camera)
It's now many months later. Still no work
from my agents. I've written and directed a
low-budget feature for Playboy . . . but no
real money. Since Stigmata came out eight
months ago and was the number one picture in the country, I have made under ten
thousand dollars as a screenwriter.

EXT. LAZARUS MANSION - NIGHT

Lazarus walks with his hounds.

TITLE: MANY MONTHS LATER

Lazarus talks into CAMERA.

LAZARUS
My agents have set up a bunch of meetings
that have been very positive and they've
just done a wonderful negotiation with

Playboy for me to produce, write and direct
their first weekly series, and I'm about to
start directing another feature.
                    (smiling)
I'm officially happy with my agents.

He throws a ball for the dogs and continues on
his walk.

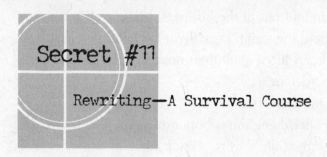

Secret #77

Rewriting—A Survival Course

> "Rewriting is the challenge of the Gods."
> —Deborah Dean Davis, WGA *Journal*

Okay, you've done your scene list, log line, then sat down and wrote your script.

There, wasn't that easy?

You took some chances, stayed pretty close to the story you planned and have, somehow, magically, come out with ninety-five pages of what you proudly tell yourself is a pretty damn good, relatively short draft.

First, enjoy your victory. You did it! You actually finished a rough draft of your script. You're a writer and it feels good.

Salinger, Nabokov, Philip Roth, You! All writers! Go on and celebrate . . . for about a day.

Now's when the fun begins.

What I do is to send the rough draft, and the key is to remember, *this is the rough draft,* to a couple of readers, people in and out of the business. I don't tell them anything about the script. I ask them for notes. When I hear from them, I listen to all their notes and do my damndest not to be defensive.

It's hard to hear criticism.

Even after doing this a bunch of years, I still have difficulty. After all, they're criticizing my universe. I've forced myself to understand they're not criticizing me, they're criticizing my script, and it's all part of the process. And, honestly, there are times I still get bent out of shape and act like a jerk.

I list all of their notes, then evaluate them. Some of them are terrific and give me new ways to think about my script. Some of them make no sense whatsoever and I discard them with thanks.

Now I have a final list of **Rewrite Notes.**

I've been away from the script for a while and the best way to get back into it is to get **a new perspective:** do another scene list, this time based on the actual script.

Inevitably, I've edited and revised the scene list as I wrote the rough draft. New scenes, new twists, new evolutions of the story came to me and they've changed the scene list.

Then I sit down and read the script.

I've forgotten parts of it, what scenes come where, and I'm hopefully reading it somewhat as my readers ultimately will. In the back of my mind, I can't help but remember the important rewrite notes.

I make indications in the script where changes will be made, but I try and read it in as close to one sitting as I can so I can get the sense of the flow.

Am I where I want to be story-wise?

Are the scenes I cut to the way I want to tell the story?

It's my logic system, but will it make sense to someone else?

When you read it, make sure you **respect your script.** Your script needs an advocate, and you are that person. It's your script, you don't have to please all your readers. It has your name on it, not theirs.

When you read it, let yourself be swept away.

Don't be disappointed if it doesn't read like the Oscar winner you were sure it was.

Film writing is a process.

Your rough draft is one giant step along the way. Getting it down on paper is the toughest part and you're there. After that, the rewriting is the true fun. To make it better every time you touch it, to make it closer and closer to the idealized script you have in your mind, is pure pleasure.

I've learned over the years to tune into myself as I read,

to listen to the music of my screenplay to see what is off pitch. Now, after you've given it a respectful read, tear that puppy apart.

Change scenes. . . .

Make the dialogue sound better to your ear. . . .

Make the characters richer. . . .

Deeper . . .

Crank everything up.

Maximize the minimum you have there.

The best analogy of rewriting I know is creating a sculpture. The sculptor starts with a big raw piece of marble. The sculptor's job is to find the sculpture in the raw stone, just as your job is to find the final script in the raw pages of your rough draft.

In both the sculptor's and writer's processes, what is called for is **clarifying, polishing, bringing it out** and **maximizing** the idea into its final reality.

Rewriting is the literary equivalent of the process that takes a film rough cut and edits it into the fine cut.

It's the sophistication of the product.

When you finally trim away or change the passages that don't make sense, that are out of place, that don't sound right, logically, emotionally, in any way, then you'll be finished . . . but not done.

At this point in my writing, I still do up to ten passes to get to a revised rough draft.

I'll send it out for new comments, from different, fresh readers, then rewrite again.

How do you get readers? Pick and choose real carefully. A lot of readers don't want to hurt your feelings. You have to make it clear you're looking for notes, not support. Try and find a writer. Try and find someone who likes to read.

A Personal Rant

If you've ever been asked to read someone else's work and give notes, a tip: **criticize within the context of their screenplay**. I'm tired of criticism like "I think instead of the romantic comedy you wrote, I think it should be an action/adventure movie. Think *Gladiator* meets *Sixth Sense*."

Spare me.

Critique what the writer is writing.

Address what's written on the page.

The best suggestions use existing material and push it to another level.

Some Other Notes on Rewriting

While rewriting, I am constantly on the prowl for **missed opportunities**, moments in my script which aren't maximized.

Maximizing is what rewriting is all about.

How can I make each scene live up to its potential? That's at the core of rewriting.

I examine each scene to see if I've fulfilled the scene's expectations.

I try and find an **internal structure** for each scene, a beginning, middle and end.

Somewhere, deep in our brains, it makes a difference reading a script on the computer monitor versus a hard-copy, on paper.

When I want to get a new perspective on the piece, I'll print a copy and do the next draft on paper. I'll read the script as it will be read. I can't really tell if a script is flowing unless I read it on paper. I think it has to do with the process, the actual page turning of reading a script.

When I'm nearing the end of the process, I'll take different passes on the script for different things. I'll read for:

> **Smooth transitions.** An important factor in the seduction of the reader/viewer.

> **The elimination of gratuitous scenes,** scenes that don't advance the plot.

> **Scene structure.** Examine the beginning, middle and end of each scene.

> **Redundancy between stage direction and the following dialogue.** A common mistake.

For example:

INT. STUDIO EXECUTIVE SUITE - DAY

The sun shines onto the aircraft carrier-sized
mahogany desk as Sweeney, SHOUTING at the
top of his lungs, throws a script at the hapless
Arthur, in the same silk shirt now unfortunately
showing the saggy nervous sweat circles under
his arms.

                    SWEENEY
          You Goddamned hack writers are all the
          same! Get out!

And the correct way:

INT. STUDIO EXECUTIVE SUITE - DAY

The sun shines onto the aircraft carrier-sized
mahogany desk as Simon throws a script at the
hapless Arthur, in a shirt that unfortunately
shows the saggy nervous sweat circles under his
arms.

                    SWEENEY
          You Goddamned hack writers are all the
          same! Get out!

Rather than write that Sweeney SHOUTS, save it for the
dialogue instead of giving it away in the stage direction.

Better drama.
Better writing.
Better.

When are you finished?
Never. Just kidding.

I consider myself finished with a screenplay when I can read through the script and don't make any real changes. A few writing cleanups. Put in the few remaining left-out words, smooth the last awkward phrases, but the length and the idea, the story dynamics of the scenes, the characters, the screenplay don't change. If it's that tight, it's finished and I'm ready to send it out.

Rewriting—An Example (Five Drafts)

Draft #1

INT. CANDLELIGHT BAR - NIGHT

A single glass of beer at the bar. Arthur holds on
to it like it's a life preserver in a tropic storm.
The Bartender, GRAFF, an ugly man with two
days worth of whiskers, eyes Arthur with concern.

GRAFF
You've had enough.

ARTHUR

Fuck you.

Graff shakes his head and goes back to washing
the glasses.

ARTHUR
(continuing)
Why do they treat us like such shit?

GRAFF

You lettum.

ARTHUR

You don't know squat.

GRAFF

I was a writer for a while.

ARTHUR

Give me a break.

GRAFF

Remember "Midnight Man"?

ARTHUR

Hey, I'm an American.

GRAFF

Well, I wrote the fuckin' thing.

ARTHUR

Yeah, and I wrote dick.

Draft #2

INT. CANDLELIGHT BAR - NIGHT

A single glass of beer at the bar surrounded by a
sea of peanut shells. Arthur sweeps the shells
onto the floor, then clutches the glass like it's a
life preserver in a tropical storm. The Bartender,
GRAFF, an ugly man with two days worth of
beard on his face and three fingers on his left
hand, eyes Arthur with concern.

                    GRAFF
     Hey, Bud, you're there.

                    ARTHUR
     Fuck you.

Graff nods and goes back to washing the glasses.

                    ARTHUR
          (continuing; into his beer)
     Why do they treat us like such shit?

                    GRAFF
     You let 'em.

                    ARTHUR
     You don't know dick.

GRAFF

I was a writer for a while.

ARTHUR

Give me a break.

GRAFF

Remember "The Bionic Man"?

ARTHUR

Hey, I'm an American.

GRAFF

Well, I wrote ten episodes of the fuckin'
thing.

ARTHUR

Why doesn't that make me feel any
better.

Draft #3

INT. CANDLELIGHT BAR - NIGHT

A glass of beer surrounded by a sea of peanut
shells. Arthur sweeps the shells onto the floor,
then clutches the glass like it's a life preserver in
a tropical storm. The bartender, GRAFF, an
ugly man with two days worth of beard, eyes Arthur with concern.

GRAFF

Hey, Bud, you're there.

Arthur doesn't look up, but knows Graff is talking to him.

ARTHUR
(tired)

Fuck you.

Graff nods and goes back to washing glasses.

ARTHUR
(continuing; into his beer)
Why do they treat us like such shit?

GRAFF
You let 'em.

ARTHUR
You don't know dick.

GRAFF
You know, I was a card-carrying writer for
a while.

ARTHUR
(suddenly more tired)
Everyone's a "writer for a while."

GRAFF

Remember "The Bionic Man"?

ARTHUR

Baseball, hot dogs, The Bionic Man.

GRAFF

I wrote ten episodes of the fuckin' thing.

ARTHUR

Why doesn't that make me feel any better.

And he downs his beer.

Draft #4

INT. CANDLELIGHT BAR - NIGHT

A glass of beer in a sea of peanut shells.
Arthur sweeps the shells onto the floor, then
clutches the glass like it's a life preserver in a
tropical storm. The bartender, GRAFF, perpetu-
ally smiling and happy, eyes Arthur with concern.

GRAFF

Hey, Artie, go home already.

Arthur doesn't look up, but knows Graff is talking to him.

ARTHUR
(tired)
Fuck you.

Graff nods and goes back to washing glasses.

ARTHUR
(continuing; into his beer)
Why do they treat me like such shit?

GRAFF
You let 'em.

Finally, Arthur looks up at him.

ARTHUR
You don't know dick.

GRAFF
You know, I was a card-carrying writer for
a while.

Arthur finishes the beer in his glass.

ARTHUR
Everyone's "a writer for a while."

Graff walks over.

GRAFF
Remember "The Bionic Man"?

ARTHUR

Who could forget?

GRAFF

I wrote ten episodes of the fuckin' thing.
How I got this place.

ARTHUR

Why doesn't that make me feel any better.

And he reaches for his beer, but his glass is
empty. Arthur looks up at Graff, who's already
pulling out another cold one.

Draft #5

INT. CANDLELIGHT BAR - NIGHT

A glass of beer in a sea of peanut shells.
Arthur drunkenly sweeps the shells onto the
floor, then clutches the glass like it's a life preserver in a tropical storm. The kickback bartender, GRAFF, eyes Arthur with concern.

GRAFF

Hey, why don't you go home already?

Arthur doesn't look up, but knows Graff is talking to him.

71

ARTHUR

Fuck you.

Graff nods and goes back to washing glasses.

ARTHUR
(continuing; into his beer)
Why do they treat me like such shit?

GRAFF

You let 'em.

Finally, Arthur looks up at him.

ARTHUR
You don't know dick.

GRAFF
I was a card-carrying screenwriter for a
while.

Arthur drains his beer.

ARTHUR
Everybody and their mother is a "screenwriter for a while."

Graff walks closer to Arthur.

GRAFF
Remember "The Bionic Man"?

ARTHUR
(sarcastic)
A fuckin' classic.

GRAFF
I wrote ten episodes of the goddamned
thing. How I got this place.

ARTHUR
Why doesn't that make me feel any better?

And he reaches for his beer, but his glass is
empty. Arthur looks up at Graff, who's already
pulling out another cold one.

Now, go back and read the original.

Each successive draft shows an incremental maximizing of the idea, the writing, the characters, the visuals.

Rewriting.

Rewriting: A Case History

After writing the dark *Christopher*, about a twelve-year-old
psychopath, I am writing something a lot lighter. It's
called *Free Love*.

I did my usual scene list and log line.

The log line: in 1967, three nineteen-year-olds from
Los Angeles travel to San Francisco for the Summer of
Love.

I'm very excited about this idea as I've always wanted to write a '60s psychedelic fairy tale of a movie.

I wail through a draft in about two weeks, writing short, writing concisely. An amazing burst of go-with-the-flow energy.

The dangers of the script are clear to me. I'm being smart. Don't make it a drug or sex movie, make it for the biggest market niche — twelve- to eighteen-year-olds.

So I read my draft. Unfortunately, it stinks. It's flat. The story doesn't go anywhere, the characters aren't vivid. It's on the nose, a caricature of what I wanted to write. It's awful. **On the nose** is one of the real curses of writing. It's when the characters say exactly what they mean. No subtlety, no finesse, hammer your reader/viewer over the head.

I change the title. It's now called *California Dreamin'*. Maybe the expectations for a movie called "Free Love" have something to do with it.

I chop out the redundancies, scenes that don't work, passages that don't move the story forward. I cut out the literal setup. It opened A, B, C, too straight. The form of this script should somehow reflect the time period.

It now opens with action. It's much better. I'm at eighty pages.

I read the pages from the beginning on paper, hand-write my changes, which allows me to make more detailed changes.

Writing on the computer sometimes feels too fast. The speed of the computer works against me. Handwriting slows the process down a little for me, which is a good thing.

I rewrite as I read, deepening it, moving things away from the obvious. The dialogue is too on the nose, so I cut deep. The characters, unfortunately, are saying what they're thinking, explaining things for the reader's benefit. I change that.

Good rewriting buries all that on the nose writing in subtext. I make major changes.

I now input all these changes into the computer. I don't want to get too far without reflecting the changes. I'm not rewriting Acts 2 and 3. I want to get the foundations of the script right before I move on.

I read it again. The relationships between the characters are deepening. I'm getting to know the characters. They're growing, maturing. Harder for them to reach their goals. The harder it is for your hero/heroine to reach their goal, the more heroic they are.

Then I take stock to see if I'm helping this thing or not. I think it's going well. I know better who the characters are, how they'd behave in any given situation. This maturation only comes through rewriting.

I begin to think the spine is a little straight, so I create more wrinkles in the story, turns the characters take that make it harder for them to reach their goals.

I spend more time on individual sentences and they get

richer and smoother, better written, meaning more precisely what I want them to mean.

I input these latest changes, then read pages one through twenty-one.

I yank out a three-page scene, one seventh of my opening pages, and it moves faster. You have to be ruthless. If a scene wasn't on the spine of my story, if it wasn't part of the log line, it's gone. It was also a drug scene and I don't want the script to go that way.

I write two new scenes that just flow out. I read them on the computer and again they're on the nose. I cut them dramatically and they work better. I really have to watch this tendency of writing this script on the nose. I put a reminder note on the monitor of my computer: **ON THE NOSE IS BAD!**

I'm ready to proceed to rewriting Act 2. I read it. Dialogue is still on the nose and, as always, I rewrite as I read.

I'm looking for the voice of the screenplay. My writing tends to notch in different directions depending on what I'm writing.

How scenes are constructed, how I get in and out of scenes, changes from script to script and I've yet to find the right voice for this script.

Next writing session, I write fifteen new pages and read them in the computer. I cut out yet another drug scene. This script is different. It keeps veering away from the version I've decided on.

I take a day off, then read the script from the beginning. It's simple, it's sweet, that's the good news. The bad news is it has no edge and it's flat and it's boring and I hate it.

I talk to two writer friends and run down my dilemma: I've flattened the script so I don't care about it, and the ending is a bummer. The innocence of the Summer of Love ended at the Rolling Stones concert at Altamont as a bummer. I had structured the movie the same way. Conceptually it was great, but it leaves the reader feeling bad. Not a good thing.

I reconfigure the ending. It's more up. It's better. I input all my latest rewrite notes, then read the script on paper. It's ninety pages now. I think I'm making progress.

I input the new changes and it's now eighty-seven pages. I'm happy with the changes until I read it and begin "relogic-ing" the beginning again. I move pages around, cut out more of the opening, start later and later in the story.

The opening finally works.

I continue rewriting. I am deepening and, more importantly, clarifying and sharpening the relationships. The script ends too fast, which seems to be a universal writer's problem, so I slow it down, write it more fully. On this day, instead of starting at the beginning of the script, I start at page eighty so I have a fresh head to really focus on the end.

I read the script again on paper, from the beginning. The words and meaning are more precise. I continue putting in details, put in a few more wrinkles.

The story, and this is important, is beginning to come out of the natural evolution of the characters, they're telling me how it should be. I'm finding the voice of the screenplay. My writing is becoming consistent. I feel like I know what I'm doing.

Life is good.

It's becoming a relationship script, which is what it has to be to work.

In science fiction, it often happens that the culture and cultural environment of the script overshadow the character and story. That's what was happening to my script, but it's not anymore.

Early in my career, my film editor and associate producer for a number of years always read my scripts and called me Pirandello reborn: characters in search of a story. I feel that's true with this script. It's my process and rather than fight it, I recognize and encourage it.

I read the script again concentrating on movement, visuals, putting movie into the script. I design the script visually, take a visual pass just writing the images. It's a pleasurable exercise in poetry and craft.

Now the script begins to read in its final form. Detailed and visual.

I take a couple of days off, then read the script again on paper. I'm still "precise-ing" the words, cleaning up the visual transitions between scenes.

I always keep reading without stopping, getting the flow, removing all the aberrations that break the reality of the script I'm attempting to create. It's beginning to read faster and faster, smoother and smoother.

I put the script down for a week while I direct a business management film.

Even though I work a tremendous amount—okay, the word "driven" occurred to me, but I wouldn't dare write it—I always try to have a balance in my life, something to counteract the obsessive-compulsive perfectionism I demand from my own film writing.

I do ceramics, messy, irregular, mega-gnarly things, that I never rewrite, that no one ever gives me notes on, that I'm forced to let go of so the kiln can perform its unpredictableness all over them. The freedom of letting go with my ceramics is exhilarating.

Directing always makes me feel good about myself and I come back to the script refreshed.

I pick up the script again and read it from the beginning.

I'm really disappointed. It's thin. It's not enough. It needs a "big idea," a criticism I've hated when it's been given to me, but here it seems appropriate.

What I've written is not enough.

I step back . . . time to think about it . . . get a little room. Examine what I'm doing and what I feel about it.

I give it to my wife, Stevie, also a film writer. She agrees with me. The script is "not much."

I think of solutions.

I open up my head. I allow in new thoughts, new combinations, new solutions. I go back to making notes, not censoring any idea, allowing myself to take chances again . . . and then it comes. . . .

It's party time! I have an idea. I have the big idea! I use a film-writing style I've been developing . . . so I script in interviews, mixed film techniques, layered, nonlinear storytelling.

Drugs are in! Sex is in! Am I selling out? God, I hope so.

Now I feel I'm on the right track. I wrote "their" movie, now I'm going to write "my" script. And I write like a madman.

I'm excited and add a ton of stuff, cut out a ton of stuff and I'm at 101 pages. I read it twice in a row, real fast.

It's good. I'm stoked. It's working for me. I read it again. Input the changes and give it to Stevie to read again. She reads it real fast. It works!

Her notes are good: one of the three main characters works a hundred percent, emotional, surprises, he's done. The other two main characters need work. I totally agree.

I'm on the right track.

I've saved the script. I've snatched it from the jaws of defeat.

"I'd like to accept this Oscar on behalf of all the starving, unwashed writers out there. . . ."

DISSOLVE TO:

FOUR MONTHS LATER . . .

After directing my screenplay, *Word of Mouth*, for Playboy's Mystique Productions, I come back to *California Dreamin'* . . .

. . . and hate it.

Not enough.

On the nose.

Predictable.

I try rethinking it, going back again to the roots of the idea, examining why I had written what I had written, what I had liked about the idea originally. I check my notes, my original inspiration . . .

. . . **then I abandon it**.

Throw it away.

In the garbage.

With little or no regret. I don't feel I did anything wrong. I don't beat myself up for not finishing it. I tried. It didn't work. I'm allowed. Maybe one day I'll come back to it.

At least I've got my health.

Secret #12

Cut to the Heart of the Scene

INT. STUDIO CONFERENCE ROOM - DAY

Looking hungover and a little disheveled, Arthur
Pratt enters. Simon Sweeney's at the door to
meet him.

          SWEENEY
The A man.

          ARTHUR
Hi, Simon . . .

Sweeney motions to the people sitting around
the conference table.

SWEENEY

I don't think you know everyone . . .this is
Teddy Cee . . .

Arthur shakes Teddy's hand.

SWEENEY
(continuing)

This is Stephanie.

Another handshake.

SWEENEY
(continuing)

Joyce . . .

Arthur smiles.

SWEENEY
(continuing)

John . . .

Arthur nods.

SWEENEY
(continuing)

Jennifer . . .

Arthur smiles.

SWEENEY
(continuing)
And Matthew.

Sweeney holds up Arthur's script. Almost all of
the page corners are dog-eared.
Arthur sags down into a chair and steels himself
for the attack.

SWEENEY
(continuing)
We all read it . . . and . . . let's get to work.

Don't have people endlessly introducing each other at the
beginning of a meeting.

Don't have characters discuss the weather ad nauseam
before you get to the reason the scene exists.

**Cut right to the action, the information load of the
scene.**

I learned about cutting to the heart of a scene in the
editing room.

Study how films are edited . . . it'll help your writing. Think
how what you're watching would appear on the page.

If our job as writers is to seduce the reader, we don't
do that by having people walking through doors, climbing

stairs, knocking at the door, introducing themselves to the receptionist, the secretary, finally, the boss, the boss' assistant, then finally getting down to what the scene is about. The reader/viewer is a lot hungrier for real information than that.

Fill sucks.

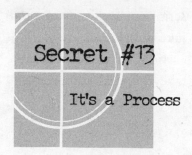

Secret #13

It's a Process

Real important.

You don't have only one chance when you write your script. It takes a lot of work, hour after hour, day after day, week after week and it's key to understand that no single piece of writing on any given day is vital.

Keep moving forward.

If I have a dry day, I have a dry day. I will write nonetheless, keep moving forward. There are many days to come where my writing will make up for this momentary lapse. It's vital to keep writing. No one session of your writing is precious. Or a matter of life and death.

Take chances, try something, allow yourself to make

mistakes. No one's watching. No one's judging. It's just you and your script . . . no mistakes here.

When you're finished is the time to worry about mistakes. When you send your script out to agents or producers or your parents, then start worrying.

During the process of film writing, because it's made up of little stabs of writing, **take chances**. Let the story tell itself.

Trust your story.

Don't write according to formula to sell.

Find your own voice.

Take chances.

Trust these wild ideas that pop into your head.

Trust the ideas you're afraid of.

Trust the ideas that embarrass.

Trust the truths, the fears that you confront in the course of getting in touch with what you're really writing about.

Embrace the unknown.

Take the shot.

You can always change it back.

When I was hiring freelance writers to write episodes on a few of the television shows I worked on, I would always look for writers with original voices, writers who would take chances, write weird or quirky or eccentric.

· · ·

Formula writing is boring writing.

Give your personal, unique voice a chance to come out. Film writing is subjective.

There is no single right solution to any creative problem. Trust yourself.

Allan Ginsberg, the poet, said about first drafts:

"The first thought is the best."

Ernest Hemingway said:

"The first draft of anything is shit."

Secret #14

It's About Character, Stupid

We access a story, a movie, a script through character. It's how we relate, sympathize, it's how we feel, by identifying with the feelings of the characters. It's how we as reader/viewers plug in, get seduced. So who your characters are and how you write them is one of the most important things you can do in the creation of your script.

Characters move the story.

Their progress, most times, is the movement of your story.

They provide the engine to your movie.

Characters experience conflict in trying to achieve their goals, in interaction with other characters, and interacting with themselves. That conflict is what drama/storytelling is all about, the stuff movies are made of.

Characters are more interesting when not only do they make things happen, but things happen to them.

A nice way to think about a character's relationship to the story is: **situation pushes character, character pushes situation.**

Characters need particular points of view.

They need to be one of a kind.

When creating characters, the danger is in creating the hooker with a heart of gold, or the luscious young daughter of a farmer, the greedy industrialist willing to step all over the environment for his own personal benefit, or the darling old homeless lady who really is worth eight kazillion dollars.

We've all seen them.

We've all written them.

The rule is: don't.

How do you make a character unique? By **particularizing** a character rather than writing a generic one.

The most common mistake? Modeling characters we've seen or heard on radio and television and film. Other writers' characters.

Bring something new to your characters. You know people who are unique. Harvest the uniqueness of your friends and acquaintances and appropriate the best of it in your characters.

Look around . . . individualized behavior is all around you. Looking for interesting characteristics legitimizes looking at people if you're into that sort of thing. I am. I study people, how they dress, what they say, how they stand, how they combine clothes, comb their hair, respond to different situations.

I also study myself, try to get in touch with my processes, my personal psychology, and incorporate these characteristics into my characters.

Ultimately, you will write you anyway. Get in touch with the characters inside of you, the different facets of you.

One of the odder things about my writing is that I seem to gravitate toward writing proactive young woman characters. While doing this rewrite, I'm also finishing up a new screenplay, *Butterfly*, the story of a young woman who dreams of being a cop and being in love. I'm able to write these women characters because I'm able to get in touch with the feelings inside of me that parallel the characters' journey through their emotions. Being in touch with myself allows me to get in touch with my characters.

The ability to get in touch with truths, feelings, emotions and experiences inside of each of us, and the ability to get them out and onto the page is one of the definitions of being a writer.

One way to better, more layered characters is to create character biographies.

ARTHUR PRATT—late forties, is a distant relative of the publishing Pratts of Philadelphia. Arthur was a violinist in high school, on the debate team and a boy who lived pretty much in his head rather than being a jock like his older brother Richard. Richard ended up selling shoes less than a mile from the house he grew up in. Arthur went to Cornell, where he learned to drink seriously and ended up editor of the humor magazine. He was notorious for his double entendres and was suspended for two issues his senior year. Everyone said Arthur should be a comedy writer in Hollywood or on *Saturday Night Live*. They kind of all took it for granted. It was a sure thing.

Arthur moved to Hollywood after graduation and within three months had married an actress named Jillian. They were divorced after six months. He had married after knowing her three weeks.

When instant success didn't happen, Arthur fell into serious drinking and drug taking. Any jobs he did get, and he got a few, the money went to support his growing habits.

Arthur struggled for six years, a couple of episodes here and there, but no real success.

Arthur lives alone in an apartment near Park La Brea. He reads paperbacks and mysteries from the public library.

He struggles with his weight, his wardrobe, his appearance, depression and staying straight.

He pulls at the hair in his ear.

He feels like he's slowly fading from sight.

He has two children's fat-tired electric cars he races around the apartment.

He has two or three friends, acquaintances really, that are pretty much like him, failed writers, and most of all, Arthur is desperate.

Give your characters identifying idiosyncrasies, habits, tics, speech repeats, particular vocal eccentricities and patterns, something that sets that character apart from your other characters.

A little here goes a really long way.

The downside of this, of course, is if your characters become a gallery of twitching, tic-ing, peculiar characters we can't relate to.

After a while, you'll know who they are so you'll know how they'll react when they're surprised by circumstances beyond their control.

One of the most important secrets for writing great characters is **the Character Arc**. It's a development cliché, but, nonetheless, worthwhile.

The character arc is the journey your character goes on.

He or she should start in one place and end up in another.

Along the way, your character learns something, has

character-testing experiences, and finds themselves in a new and better place . . . sounds like a movie to me.

Another way to create great characters is to **know what your characters need**, what they want, what's their goal.

Master film writer Robert Towne, who wrote *Chinatown* among other wonderful screenplays, asks his characters "What are they afraid of?"

It's all a way to get deeper into your characters.

If you know your character's goals and write the spine of your script only about them, and your character ends up in a better place by following what they believe in and controlling their destiny, odds are your script is going in the right direction.

PUT YOUR MAIN CHARACTER IN THE CENTER OF THE MOVIE.

We access the story through the main character.

We want to see the movie through the main character's eyes.

Keep the main character in the center of your script.

In the center of all the key scenes.

Let us see and hear the main character's reactions to events.

He or she shouldn't be on the sidelines.

We pay the actor who plays the lead the most money and we want to see him front and center.

I've mentioned a script I wrote called *Breaking Story*

for NBC. They told me the project was the archetypical movie of the week for them and that they were going to send my presentation to all their major suppliers.

This was the one.

As I said previously, after I did a draft, the network, in its infinite wisdom, brought in an Old Pro to rewrite me when the new executive assigned to the project didn't feel I was "right" for it.

This Old Pro has a wonderful reputation. He was just going to do "a polish," said the producer on the picture, "a little polish."

Well, it turns out, the Old Pro didn't like the script much, so, given the opportunity to write on my script, he threw out a number of the major story elements and squeezed in an interest of his . . . the Internet. It was in the news, why not pounce on it?

Apparently for the story to work, the old pro created a key character who was a college professor by day and a garbage man by night.

Excuse me?

A college professor/garbage man?

Seems that's what it took to make the story work.

That was, once again, a college professor/garbage man.

The network ultimately passed on the project.

I know in my heart they passed because of characters like that . . . and I don't blame them.

• • •

DOES YOUR MAIN CHARACTER HAVE TO BE LIKABLE?

It helps.

Some of the screen's most memorable characters have been unlikable. Conventional wisdom would say yes, they have to be likable . . . but . . .

I'm from the other school. I write characters who interest me, who fascinate me and will hopefully fascinate the reader/viewer as well. I have forty unproduced screenplays.

Character Description

The introduction of your characters is very important. How you describe them the first time, and every time, is vital to our relating to and understanding your characters.

There are two different schools of thought on character description.

One group of writers thinks you only describe what kind of person the character is.

The other school thinks you only describe what we can see, i.e., how the character dresses, the color of their hair, their physical type.

The former group argues that if you describe your character as portly and bald, and Leonardo DeCaprio wants to play him, what do you do?

My advice?

Cast DeCaprio and rewrite the script.

I used to write just the physical description. I never wanted to put description like "ambitious" because that was cheating, there's no way a director can film that he's "ambitious" . . . but, now, I've taken a middle ground and am using a little of both. Whatever best sells the character to the reader. Whatever best services your screenplay. There is no cheating.

Make sure your character descriptions are memorable without calling attention to themselves.

Here's an example of good character description from Scott Alexander and Larry Karaszewski's wonderful screenplay, *Ed Wood*:

> Pacing nervously in the rain is ED WOOD, 30, our hero. Larger-than-life charismatic, confident, Errol Flynn-style handsome, Ed is a human magnet. He's a classically flawed optimist: Sweet and well intentioned, yet doomed by his de- mons within.

Nice. I love good writing.

Here are some other examples:

> She's DR. LACY KENDRICKS, 30's, as beauti- ful as she is brilliant, much more intense than

Allan, in a turtleneck with a flannel shirt over it, jeans, hiking boots.

Here the wardrobe helps describe who the character is.

MATTHEW HARDAWAY is a handsome man. Mid-thirties, expensively dressed in a Brooks Brothers button-down shirt, pressed jeans and hand-tooled, ostrich Tony Lamas.

The wardrobe helps here as well.

SLOW MOTION of a formally-dressed horse show audience watching FRANK LLOYD WRIGHT, 37, striking, with radically long hair over his collar, wearing a custom-tailored riding habit and a flamboyantly flowing tie, leading Kano, an incredible black mare, around the ring.

LOIS RYDER, America's Darling, among Hollywood's most glamorous women and Olympia Studios' biggest star, in a short-sleeved sweater and pleated slacks, with her shoulder-length auburn hair over one eye, bursts out of the bathroom with a broad smile and strikes a "Here I am" pose.

OSCAR DEENE, wearing a stained robe and
barefoot, is sprawled like some kind of huge
bearded whale on the rug. He is very dead.

GABE SUMMERS, handsome, 40, in just
Jockey shorts, doing the funky chicken with absolute total abandon.

Describe major characters more than you describe mi-
nor characters.

SHANNON, an odd-looking woman in her fifties.

MORRIS, a man with an unfortunate drool.

DETECTIVE FORBES, a hard-nosed man in
shirtsleeves with a lethal-looking back 9mm Ber-
etta in his leather shoulder holster.

You get the idea.

The Protagonist

The hero.
The character we invest in the most.
The character who moves the story, who makes things
happen.

Proactive protagonists make things happen. That's who we want our heroes to be. We like and care about proactive main characters.

Reactive protagonists don't move the story. They do what other people suggest. Things happen to them. They're nowhere near as interesting or as much fun.

The best protagonists are proactive.

I was asked to consult on a script written by another screenwriting teacher. I was flattered. It was an interesting story, but terminally flawed because the writer had not put the unfortunately reactive protagonist, our hero, in the center of the story. People walked over to our hero and volunteered clues, when he should have gone out and tracked them down himself.

When there was a hair-raising chase, the protagonist, our hero, wasn't the one chased, wasn't the one in jeopardy. He was told about it later on.

When there was a love scene, the protagonist was not the seducer.

In the dramatic climax, the protagonist was watching the action through binoculars.

And in the very end, when the protagonist finally raced to save the girl, he failed and she died.

My hero.

The Antagonist

The bad guy.

He or she keeps your protagonist from reaching their goal.

A smart, formidable antagonist makes the hero earn his or her money. That's good.

The rule is: the badder the Bad Guy the gooder the Good Guy.

Actors love to play bad guys because oftentimes they're memorable, with quirky colors.

Because we've seen so many colorful bad guys in our lives on movies and TV, in plays and on the news, the Snidely Whiplash, mustache-twirling antagonist doesn't cut it anymore.

Bad guys today can be anything: nice, kindly, stoic, manic psychotic, anywhere your mind takes you to create a bad guy we haven't seen before.

It's not a bad idea to do a character biography on the antagonist. The better you know them, the better they will be as characters.

Focus on the arc of the antagonist so his opposition to the hero isn't one-noted. Like everything else, if you don't give the reader/viewer different and more interesting behavior from your antagonist, they will tune out.

A memorable bad guy is reason enough to make a movie.

Secret #15

Dialogue

Read your dialogue out loud.

What sounds good to your ear is what's important.

Make sure your dialogue is "sayable." If it's sayable, it's readable.

Short dialogue blocks are good.

When a character asks a question, the other character doesn't have to answer. Characters can be on their own track. Most people don't really listen anyway, do they? Hello?

Good dialogue is not a vocabulary contest. Highfalutin' words your reader/viewer don't understand, make them feel stupid . . . not a good thing for you to do if you want them to like what they're reading or seeing.

Make your language **comfortable, conversational, easy on the ear and brain.**

Listen to a lot of conversations. Not in the media, that's the product of other writers, but when you're in a restaurant. People I eat dinner with have to get used to the fact that I'm listening to conversations at as many different tables as possible. I listen to conversations in barber shops, hot tubs, planes, at parties, airplanes, waiting rooms, elevators, anywhere I can get close and listen to people.

Dialogue—An Example

Following is an exceptional scene from the Oscar-winning screenplay by Joel and Ethan Coen of *Fargo*. The scene sets up the crime. . . .

INSIDE

The bar is downscale even for this town. Country music plays on the jukebox. We track toward two men seated in a booth at the back. One man is short, thin and young. The other man is older, dour. The table in front of them is littered with empty longneck beer bottles. The ashtray is full. Anderson approaches.

ANDERSON
I'm uh, Jerry Lundegaard. Uh, Shep Proudfoot said—

YOUNGER MAN
Shep said you'd be here at 7:30. What
gives, man?

LUNDEGAARD
Shep said 8:30.

YOUNGER MAN
We been sitting here an hour. I've peed
three times already.

JERRY
I'm sure sorry I . . . Shep told me
8:30. It was a mix-up I guess.

YOUNGER MAN
Ya got the car?

JERRY
Yah, you bet. It's in the lot there. Brand
new Ciera.

YOUNGER MAN
Yeah okay, well siddown then. I'm Carl
Rolvaag and this is my associate Gaear
Grimsrud.

JERRY
Yah, how ya doin'. So, uh, we all set on
this thing then?

CARL

Sure, Jerry, we're all set. Why wouldn't we
be?

JERRY

Yah, no, I'm sure you are, Shep vouched
for you and all. I got every confidence here
in you fellas.

They stare at him. An awkward beat.

JERRY
(continuing)
. . . So I guess that's it then. Here's the keys—

CARL

No that's not it, Jerry.

JERRY

. . . Huh?

CARL

The new Oldsmobile, plus forty thousand
dollars.

JERRY

Yah, but, the deal was, the car first see,
then the forty thousand, like as if it was the
ransom. I thought Shep told you—

CARL

Shep didn't tell us much, Jerry.

JERRY

Well, okay, it's —

CARL

Except that you were gonna be here at
7:30.

JERRY

Yah, well that was a mix-up then.

CARL

Yeah, you already said that.

JERRY

Yah. But it's not a whole pay-in-advance
deal; I give you a brand new vehicle in advance, and —

CARL

I'm not gonna debate you, Jerry.

JERRY

Okay.

CARL

I'm not gonna sit here and debate. I will
say this, though: What Shep told us didn't
make a whole lot of sense.

109

JERRY

Oh no, it's real sound, it's all worked out.

CARL

You want your own wife kidnapped.

JERRY

Yah.

Carl stares. Jerry looks blankly back.

CARL

. . . You—my point is, you pay the ransom,
what, eighty thousand bucks, I mean you
give us half the ransom, forty thousand,
you keep half, it's like robbing Peter to pay
Paul, it doesn't make any—

JERRY

Okay, it's—see it's not me payin' the ransom. The thing is, my wife, she's wealthy,
her dad he's real well off. Now I'm in a bit
of trouble—

CARL

What kind of trouble are you in, Jerry?

JERRY

Well that's, that's, I'm not gonna go inta,
inta—see I just need the money. Now her
dad's real wealthy—

CARL

So why don't you just ask him for the
money?

Grimrud, the dour older man who has not yet
spoken, now softly puts in, in a Swedish-accented
voice:

GRIMSRUD

Or your fucking wife you know.

CARL

Or your fucking wife, Jerry.

JERRY

Well, it's all just part of this— they don't
know I need it, see. Okay so there's that.
And even if they did, I wouldn't get it. So
there's that on top then. See there're personal matters.

CARL

Personal matters.

JERRY

Yah. Personal matters that needn't, uh—

CARL

Okay Jerry. You're asking us to perform this
mission but you won't uh, you won't—aw
fuck it let's take a look at that Cierra.

111

Fabulous. Tense. Funny. Surprises. I'm totally sucked in.

Dialogue—Another Example

Word of Mouth, the film I directed from my original screenplay in January 1999, had a scene where I thought the dialogue worked particularly well. The actors performed it word for word.

The setup: Darrow, a documentary filmmaker, has been interviewing Torri, the subject of his documentary, for seventy pages. Torri, a high-priced Beverly Hills call girl, finally turns the tables on him.

EXT. TORRI'S BEDROOM - NIGHT

Darrow and Pokoloff, the soundman, filming.
Torri smiling.

              TORRI
How about we try something a little different today?

Darrow looks up from his camera.

              TORRI
           (continuing)
Why don't I interview you?

Pokoloff LAUGHS.

POKOLOFF

I love it.

DARROW

I don't think so.

TORRI

I just have a few questions. It's only fair.

DARROW

This isn't a film about me.

TORRI

It's a film about us, isn't it, really?

Darrow looks over at Pokoloff, who's grinning.

DARROW

Thanks a lot.
                    (to Torri)
Okay.

Darrow climbs out from behind the camera.

DARROW
                (continuing)
It's all focused. All you have to do is . . .

TORRI
                (interrupting)
I know, I've been watching you.

Darrow sits on the chair as Torri moves behind
the camera, looks through the viewfinder, then
looks up and smiles.

                    TORRI
                  (continuing)
    Ready.

INT. TORRI'S LIVING ROOM - DAY
(DOCUMENTARY)

A smiling Darrow nods.

                 TORRI'S VOICE
                  (to Pokoloff)
    Okay, here we go.

                POKOLOFF's VOICE
    Rolling.

                 TORRI'S VOICE
    Okay . . .
                  (after a beat)
    My first question is: what exactly did you
    do for a living?

                    DARROW
    I'm a filmmaker, a documentarian.

TORRI'S VOICE
You're making a film about an escort,
right?

DARROW
I'm making a movie about an escort.

TORRI'S VOICE
You ever been to one?

DARROW
Not exactly.

TORRI'S VOICE
(LAUGHING)
Which means?

DARROW
Oh, I was at a stag party . . . years ago.

TORRI'S VOICE
And?

DARROW
There . . . there was this stripper there.

TORRI'S VOICE
This is like pulling teeth.

DARROW
And . . . you know . . . I did something with
her.

115

TORRI'S VOICE
"Something?"

DARROW
She sucked us all off.

TORRI'S VOICE
Classy.
                    (after a beat)
One last question . . . if prostitution were
legal, would you do it with me?

A long silence, then . . .

DARROW
I . . . I don't know.

TORRI'S VOICE
You have to answer in complete sentences.

Darrow LAUGHS and turns to Pokoloff.

DARROW
I'm in trouble here.

TORRI'S VOICE
If prostitution were legal would you hire
me?

DARROW
I . . . I think I probably . . . would hire you
as a . . . I would.

INT. TORRI'S LIVING ROOM - DAY
(DOCUMENTARY)

Torri smiles.

                    TORRI
How much would you be willing to pay
me?

                    DARROW
Come on.

                    TORRI
What?

                    DARROW
How much would I pay? I don't know.

                    TORRI
Would you pay a hundred dollars?

                    DARROW
Yes.

                    TORRI
Five hundred?

INT. TORRI'S LIVING ROOM - DAY
(DOCUMENTARY)

Darrow squirms.

DARROW

I . . . probably.

TORRI'S VOICE

A thousand?

DARROW

Do you take plastic?

Secret #16

Openings

The most important part of your script.

When your script is sent to a studio or producers, or to an agent for representation, more often than not it is assigned to a reader to do coverage, which is the reader's report as to what is wrong with your script and why they can't recommend it to the producer. The reader's report rates things like story, characters, plot development, commercial prospects and the like.

Professional readers are looking for reasons to find things wrong, reasons to pass. The reason? If they recommend a script to their superiors, they're going on the line with an actual opinion. What if their boss hates it? The safe way is to say no.

The challenge is to make your opening grab readers by the throat and never let go.

Here's what your opening must accomplish:

Set up story: get your story going. Antiquated structure spent the whole first act giving background, laying pipe. These days, I recommend not waiting until page thirty, but get cooking real fast, within the first ten pages. Five's even better.

Establish location: let the reader know where in the world we are, what it looks like, what it feels like.

Introduce main characters and their needs: get your main characters up and running as soon as you can. They are who we paid our money to see, so let's see them.

Establish your style: if you're going to use any particular film style — fast cuts, montages, voice-over — establish it in the early pages. Most times, I find the voice of the screenplay in the later pages. I'll have been writing; then, as time goes by, the eventual style the characters speak, the way the visuals are presented, how particularly the story is being unfolded, emerges. Then, when rewriting, I put the same voices and stylistic devices into the early pages for a consistent style.

Atmosphere: see if you can create a sense of the tone for the movie by the way you describe the weather, people's dress, the lighting, the mood. It's a subtle thing, made up of lots of little cues, of details slanted a certain way. Everything should be thought through. Every word you write must be considered, then reconsidered.

Sense of cinema: openings are one of the few places in your script where it's okay to wax cinematic. Go for the visuals as directors do in the titles. Establish a sense of cinema.

Tension: if you can create tension in your opening, a concern for the well-being of your main character, a conflict, jeopardy, then you're ahead.

Issue/theme: hopefully near the opening of your script, you'll subtly deal with the underlying issues of your script. This is a not-so-fancy term for what your movie is really about. If you don't get to your log line near the beginning, preferably within ten pages, start questioning what you're doing.

Then, after the opening . . .
Something happens:

a kidnapping,

a problem,

a mystery,

a crisis,

conflict,

a question,

a challenge,

an ultimatum . . .

any story device that kick starts the action of your script and you're off and running.

Elmore Leonard's openings: take a look at this terrific writer's work. The first few pages are rich and dense, and hook you with details and descriptions. Then, once he's got you, he relaxes his writing style and tells his story much more simply.

First time through, don't think, feel your writing, go with the flow, with your instincts. After that, think about everything. Nothing should be left unconsidered.

STIGMATA
Written by Tom Lazarus

FADE IN:

EXT. SOUTH AMERICA - DAY

Peasants, by the hundreds, rushing up a dusty
hillside. HORNS HONKING. Some peasants
hold crucifixes high in the air. Others fall,
nearly trampled by the rush of people. A dusty
Land Rover, led by an even dustier Police vehicle, HONKS as it moves slowly through the
hordes of people heading up the hillside.
Surrounded by a crush of people, some praying,
some crying, the door to the Land Rover opens
and ANDREW, thirties, good looking, in dusty
khakis and hiking boots, carrying a palm-sized
video camera over his head, pushes through the
multitude.

EXT. HILLSIDE - THROUGH VIDEO
CAMERA - DAY

Andrew's followed by two MEN IN HARD
HATS and Day-Glo vests and a young Catholic

123

priest. Andrew makes it through the people, most SINGING a Spanish Catholic hymn, to the top of the hill . . .

. . . to a two-lane highway . . . and the cliff next to it where there's a small stone niche housing a statue of the Virgin of Guadalupe. The peaceful face on the Virgin is golden, unlike the rest of the figure or the surrounding rocks. Bunches of handpicked flowers and devotionals surround the modest shrine. Andrew videotapes . . .

THROUGH VIDEO CAMERA

Peasants praying, then ZOOMING IN to the face of the Virgin.

                    PEASANT'S VOICE
     Mi Madre . . . mi Madre. Madre mia . . .

EXT. HILLSIDE - DAY

Andrew lowers the camera moves closer to the niche and inspects it. He takes a small metal tool, reaches into the niche and carefully takes some of the gold off the Virgin's face and inspects it. His fingers touch the gold. It's wet. He shows it to one of the men in the hard hats, who looks at it through a pocket magnifying glass. Andrew points up the cliff. The man nods, then climbs up the steep cliff, looks around above the niche, then waves for Andrew and the others. The man shows Andrew a small spring trickling out between rocks, coming down from higher up the cliff side. The man leans close to Andrew, so he can be heard over the SING-ING, and talks to him in Spanish. The other Hard Hat translates.

> HARD HAT
> He says it is from the minerals in the hill, brought down by the water, the spring. It is the minerals.

> PEASANT'S VOICES
> Madre mia . . . Madre mia.

The young Priest leans close to Andrew.

> YOUNG PRIEST
> Senor, should we stop the water?
>   CUT TO BLACK.

FADE IN:

EXT. BOSTON STREET - NIGHT (TELE-PHOTO) - MAIN TITLES

The sidewalks crowded with numbed workers, bundled up against the bitter winter cold, making their way home.

EXT. BACK BAY - NIGHT - TITLES CONTINUE

Traffic racing by reveals TOBY PAGE, 23, scarf around her mouth against the wind, jaywalking off the curb and having to pull back as a huge truck THUNDERS by her.

EXT. BACK BAY - NIGHT - TITLES CONTINUE

Toby walks past a traffic jam, with cars bumper to bumper in the rush hour traffic. Drivers YELL out their windows at each other.

INT. TOBY'S APARTMENT - BATHROOM - NIGHT - TITLES CONTINUE

Toby's eyes totally and daringly made up. But behind the eyes, there's a disquietude. Toby touches gold gloss to her lips. Now fully made-up, Toby takes one last look then moves away from the mirror.

END TITLES

INT. WAREHOUSE CLUB - DAWN

Strobe lights trip. TECHNO PULSES from a
wall of monster speakers. Suspended by bungee
cords over the pierced and tattooed and undulat-
ing dancers are three nearly naked bodies, wet
with perspiration, writhing suggestively to the
heavy beat.

Another example:

BASIC INSTINCT
Written by Joe Eszterhas

FADE IN:

INT. A BEDROOM - NIGHT

It is dark; we don't see clearly. A man and
woman make love on a brass bed. There are
mirrors on the walls and ceiling. On a side table, atop a small mirror, lines of cocaine. A tape
deck PLAYS the Stones: "Sympathy for the Devil."
Atop him . . . she straddles his chest . . . her
breasts in his face. He cups her breasts. She

leans down, kisses him. JOHNNY BOZ is in his late 40's, slim, good-looking. We don't see the woman's face. She has long blonde hair. The CAMERA STAYS BEHIND and to the side of them. She leans close over his face, her tongue in his mouth . . . she kisses him . . . she moves her hands up, holds both of his arms above his head. She moves higher atop him . . . she reaches to the side of the bed . . . a white silk scarf is in her hand . . . her hips above his face now, moving . . . slightly, oh-so slightly . . . his face strains towards her. The scarf in her hand . . . she ties his hands with it . . . gently . . . to the brass bed . . . his eyes are closed . . . tighter . . . lowering hips into his face . . . lower . . . over his chest . . . his navel. The SONG plays. He is inside her . . . his arms tied above him . . . on his back . . . his eyes closed . . . she moves . . . grinding . . . he strains for her . . . his head arches back . . . his throat white. She arches her back . . . her hips grind . . . her breasts are high . . . Her back arches back . . . back . . . her head tilts back . . . she extends her arms . . . the right comes down suddenly . . . the steel flashes . . . his throat is white . . . He bucks, writhes, bucks, convulses . . . It flashes up . . . it flashes down . . . and up . . . and down . . . and up . . . and . . .

EXT. A BROWNSTONE IN PACIFIC
HEIGHTS - MORNING

Winter in San Francisco: cold, foggy. Cop cars
everywhere. The lights play through the thick
fog. Two Homicide detectives get out of the car,
walk into the house.
NICK CURRAN is 42. Trim, good-looking, a
nice suit: a face urban, edged, shadowed.
GUS MORAN is 64. Crew-cut, silver beard, a
suit rumpled and shiny, a hat out of the '50s: a
face worn and ruined: the face of a backwoods
philosopher.

INT. THE BROWNSTONE

There's money here—deco, clean, hip—That
looks like a Picasso on the wall. They check it
out.

GUS
What was this fuckin' guy?

NICK
Rock and roll, Gus. Johnny Boz.

GUS
I never heard of him.

                        NICK
                       (grins)
Before your time, pop.
                      (a beat)
Mid-sixties. Five or six hits. He's got a club
down in the Fillmore now.

                        GUS
Not now he don't.

Past the uniformed guys . . . nods . . . waves . . .
past the forensic men . . . past the coroner's in-
vestigators . . . they get to the bedroom.

INT. THE BEDROOM

They walk in, stare—it's messy. It's like a con-
vention in here. LT. PHIL WALKER, in his
50's, silver-haired, the Homicide Chief. CAP-
TAIN MARK TALCOTT, 50's, well-kept, an expensive suit: an Assistant Chief of Police. Two
homicide guys: JIM HARRIGAN, late 40's,
puffy, affable; SAM ANDREWS, 30's, black. A
CORONER'S MAN is working the bed.

                   LT. WALKER
                (to Nick and Gus)
You guys know Captain Talcott?

They nod.

GUS

What's the Chief's office doin' here?

CAPTAIN TALCOTT

Observing.

LT. WALKER

(to the Coroner's Guy)

What do you think, Doc?

THE CORONER'S GUY

The skin blanches when I press it—this
kind of color is about right for six or eight
hours.

LT. WALKER

Nobody say anything. The maid came in
an hour ago and found him. She's not a
live-in.

GUS

Maybe the maid did it.

LT. WALKER

She's 54 years old and weighs 240 pounds.

THE CORONER'S GUY

(deadpan)

There are no bruises on his body.

                    GUS
                   (grins)
It ain't the maid.

                LT. WALKER
He left the club with his girlfriend about
midnight. That's the last time anybody saw
him.

                    NICK
             (looks at the body)
What was it?

             THE CORONER'S GUY
Ice pick. Left on the coffee table in the living room. Thin steel handle. Forensics
took it downtown.

                 HARRIGAN
There's come all over the sheets — he got
off before he got offed.

                    GUS
                  (deadpan)
That rules out the maid for sure.

Terrific opening. Sexy, funny, grisly, it sure hooks me.
The characters are well and tersely described.
It cooks.

Another example:

CHRISTOPHER
Written by Tom Lazarus

FADE IN:

EXT. SCHOFIELD, NEW YORK - DAY
The sunlight is dappled and warm as it shafts
down through the sixty-foot trees shading the up-
per middle class homes. A man in jeans and a
CORNELL sweatshirt washes down his Ex-
plorer. A just-washed BMW is in the garage.
A full palette of leaves is blown by the brisk
breeze. High schoolers throw around a football.
It's autumn. America at its best.
A FRIGHTENED CHILD'S HORRIFYING
SCREAM!

EXT. SCHOFIELD STREET - DAY

CRYING children being calmed by terrified parents. A panicking MOTHER clutches her cell
phone.

MOTHER
The children are in shock . . . so
disgusting.

EXT. NEIGHBORHOOD HOUSE - DAY

A shaking child, tears on his cheeks, eyes scared,
being rushed inside. The door quickly closes behind him.

INT. DETECTIVE'S UNMARKED CAR - DAY

A concerned PLAINCLOTHES DETECTIVE,
DAN HARMON, late 20's, talks on his police
radio as he speeds along the suburban street.

DETECTIVE HARMON
I need you there now.

MAN'S VOICE
(over radio)
We'll roll after the 412 on the Saw Mill.

DETECTIVE HARMON
No. Now!

EXT. SCHOFIELD HOUSE - DAY

Ten-year-old kids drop their bikes at the curb
and excitedly run up the leaf-covered brick walk
to a large white Colonial house. When they
reach the front porch, they abruptly pull up.

                        KID
  Whoa.

They can't believe what they see.

                    ANOTHER KID
  Holy shit.

They turn away, scared, revolted.

EXT. SCHOFIELD STREET - DAY

The unmarked car SCREECHES to a stop at a
haphazard angle in front of the house. Detective
Harmon climbs out and pushes past upset parents shooing the ten-year-olds out of the yard.
He rushes up on the front porch and slams to a
stop.

DETECTIVE HARMON'S POV

To some kind of small animal that's been evis-
cerated, turned inside out, its bloody guts and
veined organs hanging down grotesquely, nailed
up on the front door for all to see.

DETECTIVE HARMON

Nauseated, has to turn away.

CUT TO BLACK.

FADE IN:

EXT. SCHOFIELD - DAY

Another brisk day. On one of the town's more rural roads, DR. TYLER LYNCH, late 30's, good looking despite needing a haircut, understated in an L. L. Bean sort of way, wearing a pager, is walking slowly with CHRISTOPHER WEEKS, a slender blonde-haired twelve-year-old in khakis, a dark blue crew neck sweater and running shoes.

                    CHRISTOPHER
          That these frogs, all around the world, are
          being born with, like, two heads, no legs,
          no eyes, eyes in the middle of their backs.
          It's, like, total freakness.

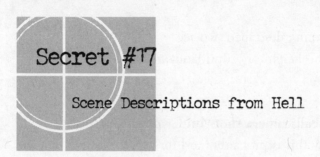

Secret #17

Scene Descriptions from Hell

One of the major causes of unreadable screenplays is poorly written, overlong scene descriptions.

There are ways to beat that.

Keep scene descriptions **brief**.

Keep them **concise**.

Make sure the words are **precise**.

Use **conversational language**.

Don't use novelistic techniques where you describe processes going on in your character's mind. There is no way a director can show that. Of course, there are ways, but it's not the way to write a script. You have to figure out how to have your characters act out their thoughts and feelings. Show rather than tell.

• • •

Don't write "We hear" or "We see."

The reason?

Everything that is spoken or heard in your script, we hear.

Everything described, we see.

It is the height of redundancy to tell us the obvious.

Do not call camera shots under penalty of death.

I know this is probably hard for you to believe, but no one really cares what you think about how you'd shoot the movie. Lots of screenwriters feel hamstrung about this . . . don't. You can accomplish the same thing as calling shots and not offend anyone.

An example, the wrong way:

INT. PRATT'S APARTMENT - NIGHT

ECU ON a cigarette burning in the nearly filled ashtray.

TIGHT ON crumpled-up typing paper. Too much of it.

PULL BACK to reveal Arthur pounding at his dirty green 1940s' WhisperTyper.

TIGHT ON a cigarette dangling from the corner of his mouth. Arthur hasn't shaved all week,
and probably hasn't showered in two.

Or, the correct way:

INT. PRATT'S APARTMENT - NIGHT

Too much crumpled up typing paper on the
floor. A cigarette burning in the nearly filled
ashtray. With another cigarette dangling from
the corner of his mouth, Arthur's pounding on
his dirty green 1940s' Smith-Corona Whisper-
Typer. Arthur hasn't shaved or showered all
week.

You accomplish the same thing and no one hates you.
Please note I couldn't help rewriting it.

Don't write dense. Design the page so it's open and accessible, so that someone wants to read it.
　　Imagine that hapless reader friend of ours carrying a
stack of scripts home for the weekend, then opening one
and finding it wall-to-wall words . . . no air, just endless,
packed stage direction describing every twitch with
nuclear-war importance.

Long weekend.

The prevailing wisdom is, don't open with page after page of dense stage direction. Skip lines wherever you can. Break huge, thick paragraphs into smaller paragraphs.

Your pages should invite reading rather than turning it away. I told all this to a student, who came to the next week's class, after having done the research, and whined that if it was all right for George Lucas to open the *Star Wars* script and Spielberg to open the *Raiders of the Lost Ark* script with pages of dense action, why couldn't she open her script that way?

I explained producers and studios will read her script differently than they will Lucas and Speilberg's. Different rules. Unfair, but true.

If you're writing all action, space it out.

Make lots of little paragraphs.

Make it easy.

White space on the page is key.

Think like a camera, but don't call the shots.

One of my big complaints with scene description writing is that the scenes often aren't written with an underlying logic of seeing.

A couple of things to think about:

> **Write what the camera sees**. It goes from tight
> shot to wide shot, left to right, from exterior to
> interior.

Your description should end on the action, or the character who will be speaking. This is vital for screenplays to read well. One of the keys to good flow writing, writing that is smooth and seamless, is that scene description ends where you're going, where the next focus is.

The wrong way:

INT. SWEENEY'S OFFICE - DAY
Simon Sweeney sits at his desk fingering a script with the corners turned down. The sun shafts fall across the office. Arthur Pratt squirms uncomfortably in the chair across from the desk.

                    SWEENEY
          Arthur, it's not me, but there are people at
          the studio who just don't get it.

There is no logic to the above description. It makes no sense. First we see Sweeney, then the script, the sun, Arthur and back to Sweeney for his dialogue.

Here's the correct way:

INT. SWEENEY'S OFFICE - DAY
The sun shafts fall across the office. Arthur Pratt squirms uncomfortably in the chair across from

the desk. Fingering a script with the corners
turned down at his desk, Simon Sweeney smiles.

SWEENEY
Arthur, this is brilliant. We're going to
shoot it as is.

See, Simon Sweeney even liked the script better.

Secret #18

Endings

Running for the barn.

Rounding the last corner and heading home.

They both mean you'll soon be writing . . .

FADE OUT.

THE END.

. . . and it's going to feel great.

The natural inclination is to write the ending too fast. You're near the end, you can smell it, so you rush through everything just to get there. Everyone does it at one time or another.

Don't resist.

Let yourself be drawn into the excitement of the finish . . . getting to the end is what's important. Go with the flow. Write with real energy. Make the reader feel the excitement. Then write FADE OUT.

THE END.

Take a few bows . . . then, before anyone gets a chance to read your mess . . .

Rewrite it. Add the grace notes. Play out the beats. Maximize the scenes.

Then you'll really be finished.

Try to have your ending somehow relate to the opening.

It's always a nice thing when the ending resonates with pipe you've laid down in the opening. It gives the reader/ viewer a wondrous sense of satisfaction and closure. Sometimes it doesn't work that way, but it's worth a try.

Endings should answer all questions, tie up all loose ends.

The ending is the climax of the rising action, the end of the A story, the spine.

It's the final destination in your character's journey.

The end is the epiphany where your protagonist is enlightened.

One of the problems we have with endings is how to tie up the multiple stories you've been weaving. My advice is to **prioritize** them. Start your endings with the least important, saving the most important, the ending of the spine story, the ending of the protagonist's journey, for the absolute climax.

The Pitfalls

Here are some of the common mistakes, perpetrated by us all:

> **Anticlimaxes:** This is when you end, then add another ten anticlimactic pages to tie up loose ends. After the final climax, get out while the getting out is good.
>
> **Premature ejaculation:** not playing out the moment. It's all over too fast. An unmaximized ending.
>
> **Running for the barn:** when you're out of control going for the fade out. Slow down. There's no hurry. Write the closing as many times as you write your opening. They're equally important.
>
> **Morris the Explainer:** you know Morris, he's the guy who comes in at the end of your script to explain all the things you haven't written clearly enough in the body of the script. Resist the temptation. Don't depend on Morris to excuse your less-than-perfect writing. Work harder.

Hollywood Endings? Many writers are scared of happy endings. Something about being uncool, about selling out. They should be so lucky. Don't worry about writing happy endings, **write satisfying endings**. Try to get to the heart of the issues/feelings/journey that your character is involved in.

In the Julius and Harry Epstein script, *Casablanca*, we wanted Bogart and Bergman to end up together, but when they didn't, we were still satisfied. Why?

Good storytelling. And they played out the ending. We as the audience could cry and feel for the characters and thereby move on to the new and better place they got to (character arc).

Keep exploring alternate endings. It's great to start a script with an ending in place. But don't get locked into it. Let yourself be open.

Let your story or characters tell you what the ending should be.

Remain open to your story evolving in surprising ways.

Secret #19

All the Other Stuff

Okay, those are the eighteen big secrets of film writing. But there are more ideas and thoughts and, dare I say, insights that can make you a better writer and your screenplay a better read.

Surprises, Wrinkles, Twists and Turns

A script that doesn't contain any surprises, or wrinkles, twists and turns is predictable.

Predictable is bad and no one will buy your script. You will be selling shoes. Fade to black.

Well, not exactly, but you get the point.

. . .

The best screenplays bring something new, a new slant, a different way of telling the same story.

If the reader/viewer is not surprised, is not kept on the edge of their seats on some level, they will check out of your script, they won't care.

If they guess where the story's going, you're road kill.

Do it or die.

Text Versus Subtext

For me, the toughest concept to communicate is subtext. And, it's real important.

An example:

One day, the man who delivers my newspaper in the morning left me this handwritten note.

> I have been your New York Times carrier.
> I want to give you my best service, for
> that reason if you have any question or
> any problem with my service please call
> me. Or if you don't get the paper for
> any reason call me and I will take you a
> paper immediately.
> I am doing that because I want to save
> problems in my job and I don't want to
> lose my job.
> I am ready to attend you 24 hours a day.

Thanks for your attention.
I love my job.

That kind man wrote the **subtext** into his note. Exactly what he meant.

The **text** is:

If you have questions or problems, give me a call and I'll take care of it.

The subtext is:

I don't want to lose my job.

Text is what you say.

Subtext is what you really mean.

Characters that don't say exactly what they mean are much more interesting.

Using the Wrong Words

I've mentioned these before, they bear repeating. We're all waiting for Spellchecks to be sophisticated enough to catch the misuse of the following:

Their, there, they're.

It's, it is, its.

Your, you're.

Lets, let's.

Lay and lie.

Affect and effect.

To, too, two.

I recommend before you send out the script, do a search in your screenplay for any of the above words and when you find them, examine them carefully so that you're using the correct one.

Check words you're not sure of in a dictionary . . . a real one, made out of paper and everything.

It's hard to get a fresh perspective on your screenplay. Takes a lot of focus.

One of my better students had a propensity for using the wrong word. My favorite:

> To quiet the boisterous courtroom, the judge
> pounded his anvil.

Phone Conversations

Try to keep phone conversations in your screenplay to a minimum.

Having your characters in two different locations is inherently undramatic.

Putting both sides on the screen via a split screen is worse. The manipulation of the screen that presents an

out-of-the-norm, you-have-to-think-about-it image breaks
the seduction you're working so hard to sustain.

Having your characters interact in the presence of each
other is more dramatically satisfying.

How to write a phone conversation:

INT. SIMON SWEENEY'S BEDROOM - NIGHT

Simon and his WIFE, a young silicone queen,
sleep to the HUM of the air conditioner. The
PHONE RINGS. Simon grabs the phone before it can ring again.

                    SIMON
Sweeney.

                ARTHUR'S VOICE
                (through the phone)
Your wife there?

                    SIMON
Who the hell is this?

INT. BAR - NIGHT - INTERCUT AS
DESIRED

A drunken Arthur leans against the wall talking
on the pay phone.

ARTHUR

Arthur Pratt. I've solved the third act.

SIMON

It's two in the morning!?

ARTHUR

What day?

Signs of an Amateur

Bad format. The sure sign of a nonprofessional. The last thing any writer wants is for a reader to pick up their script and think they're an amateur. It happens every time a writer "invents" his own format. Don't do it. Ever. Refer to the example of perfect format earlier in the book.

Vomiting. There was a time in the early '90s that every American movie I saw and every script I read had a vomiting scene. Too many still do. What are these writers thinking? This is entertainment? I was and still am repulsed by on-screen vomiting. Granted, this is more than likely a very personal issue but this is my book and I get to talk about this. If you write vomiting scenes, your script will never sell and you'll rot in Hell.

Missing Words. Another problem not found by Spellcheck. It takes the most careful kind of proof reading to catch all the little words you forget and leave out. Take a pass just to check on missing words. It's real tough to proof your own script. A second set of anal-compulsive eyes is a real plus.

No stage direction after slug lines. A sure sign of the amateur. Every slug line, which is:

INT. SIMON SWEENEY'S OFFICE - DAY

Must be accompanied by a scene description, which is:

Simon paces as he talks on his earset phone.

The reason? That's the way it's done. It reinforces the visual, gives the director something to shoot.

Movies are made of images that move. I find that scenes that last more than three pages are very suspect.

Many inexperienced writers write long, long, maybe eight- to ten-page scenes.

One-and-a-half-page scenes are great.

Two-page scenes are good.

Three-page scenes are right on.

Four-page scenes are suspect.

Five-page scenes are too long.

Six-page scenes are potentially embarrassing.

Seven-pages scenes are abusive.

Eight-page scenes are self-destructive.

Nine pages are criminal.

Ten pages are suicidal.

Flagging Problems

If something is troubling, some piece of logic, something about the story that bothers you, rather than trying to hide it, have one of your characters flag it for you.

They will mention in dialogue the exact thing that's worrying you as the writer.

The classic is probably the noir masterpiece *To Have and Have Not*.

The story was so complicated, with so many characters, so many twists and turns, that the filmmakers were concerned that people were going to be lost; so they flagged the problem, and wrote a scene where one of the characters sits on the desk in the police chief's office and tells us who's done what to who for the last hour.

Problem over.

It will feel like cheating, but it's not.

Well, maybe it is, but it's better than ignoring the problem. A problem in the rough draft, left unsolved, will end up a problem in the editing room.

The Writer's Mantra

In talking to many writers over the years, I've discovered one of the little-discussed aspects to our process of creation is the mantra that goes around in our heads as we sit down to write.

Most writers, it seems, have mantras like:

INT. ARTHUR'S APARTMENT - NIGHT

Arthur's fingers are frozen on the typewriter keys.

                    ARTHUR
                  (voice over)
      Why would anyone read this junk? It
      stinks. I stink. I've got a helluva nerve even
      thinking for one second that these measly
      words I scrawl are even worthy of wrapping
      fish. I should be ashamed . . . . I am
      ashamed. I'm not worthy.

On the other hand, the mantra that ricochets around in my noggin is:

INT. WRITER'S MOUNTAIN RETREAT - DAY

A few days of whiskers burring his mug, Lazarus's fingers are flying on keyboard of his laptop.

LAZARUS
(voice over)
This is great! The words just sing. It's incredible. I'm incredible. I'd like to accept this
Oscar on behalf of my brother and sister
writers who toil in the fields of Hollywood.

You can control what your mantra is . . . control it so it
helps and supports your writing.

Pitching—Six Minutes of Hell

"Scripts deal with characters, pitches deal with concepts."
—Ron Shelton, *film writer*

Pitching: the verbal presentation of a story or idea in
hopes of selling it before actually writing it.

It all starts with ideas.

I come up with what I want to write next. I work out
the idea, then call my agent and say I've got a pitch.

I pitch them, then their excitement translates into
meetings . . . with producers who might be interested in
the financing of the script/series/movie of the week.

The agents don't tell them any of the idea . . . just that
it's me . . . what my credits are and what I've been doing
recently. The producers sometimes want a sample of my
writing beforehand . . . definitely afterwards.

The given: development people and producers have the attention span of a maggot.

Therefore, you've got to be prepared to get in, get on and get out in **six minutes**.

When you arrive in their office, look around for something to talk about. Sometimes I'll choose what's hanging on their walls. That'll comprise **the schmooze**. Two or three minutes of this is fine. It's important. If you don't talk about art, you can talk about the latest scandal, divorce or face lift. It's all the same . . . meaningless social graces. "How 'bout those Lakers?" I stink at it. I'm so keyed up and focused on the pitch, I want to start pitching as I walk in the door. To hear about a producer's triplets' rash. Spare me.

Now it's time . . . what do you pitch?

Luckily, you're well prepared with a verbal pitch and a **leave behind:** two to four, maybe six pages of your pitch, written down, so if the person you're pitching likes it, they can take it to their boss and pitch it, rather than trying, to the best of their addled memories, to recreate what you pitched them. You hand it to them . . . typed, of course, perfectly.

Here's how to create your pitch.

If you haven't written the piece you're pitching, you have to figure out the following elements and put them in the pitch:

The main character and his or her journey.

The beginning, middle, and end of three acts.

The major beats, the big scenes, the ones that'll appear in the trailer.

The reason to make the movie.

I once pitched a caper movie called *10 Million Ben Franklins*. A few minutes into the pitch, after I had given the basic idea of the movie, the good guy and the bad guy, I showed the producer a thirty-second video of the actual location of the caper, a five-story underground vault. The producer went crazy.

PRODUCER
Incredible! The reason to make this movie.

I script my pitch.

I type what I have: the story, the characters under the heading **PITCH NOTES**, and bring a clean copy as my leave behind.

Calling the leave behind PITCH NOTES is a hedge . . . so the producer won't think the pages are a treatment or presentation . . . though, of course, that is exactly what they are.

Telling the pitch through the main character and **giving the arc of the main character.**

Mention the antagonist if you have a good one.

When I have my pitch together, I pitch anyone I can get a hold of.

Someone asks me what I'm doing, I tell them I'm working on a project . . . and launch into my pitch.

Sometimes my friends run when they see me approach.

It helps me to keep pitching, so when I get into my pitch meeting, with the pitch notes on my lap, I'll damn near have the pitch memorized.

The key is you have to **work your idea all the way out to pitch the essence of it.**

As much as anything else, in a pitch you're selling:

> **PASSION** — Executive and development people
> want to say no. It makes their life easier to say
> no; then they won't be judged by their mistakes.
> For economic reasons, the number of yeses has
> to be small. They're swayed by the depth of the
> passion of the writer doing the pitch. You have
> to convince them this is the one, the big one;
> and you, and only you, are the writer to write it.

> **COMPETENCE AND PROFESSIONALISM** —
> In the middle of your pitch, the development
> person or producer is already thinking who'd be
> good to rewrite you, so your job is to convince
> them you have the total handle on this idea,

know what you're doing, are going to be easy to work with and even might be fun. You have to convince them by your grasp of the material, of the levels at which you've thought about it and your flexibility when they suggest something. You're looking to have a partner in this project. If you accept some of their ideas, suddenly they're invested in the project and you have a better chance of getting a deal. Try not to grovel. Try to keep a shred of your dignity.

ENTHUSIASM — Convince them you care about this idea more than life itself, that you were born to write this script and nothing, *nothing*, will stop you from reaching your goal. Showing a little blood isn't a bad idea.

Should you pitch more than one idea?

Not sure.

On one hand it vitiates your absolute belief in one idea but, on the other hand, it increases your odds of selling something.

When I was younger, I would pitch only one idea. Now, I've been talking about three projects during a pitch: one finished script, one script I'm writing and, finally, the script I'm researching. It's probably a sign of desperation. Oh, well.

If I'm pitching just one idea, I usually have a second

pitch in my hip pocket when, after the first thirty seconds
of pitching the development exec says the inevitable . . .

> DEVELOPMENT EXEC
> Sorry, we have a project like that in devel-
> opment . . .

Or . . .

> DEVELOPMENT EXEC
> (continuing)
> I love it, but I can't sell it to Sherry. . . .

Or . . .

> DEVELOPMENT EXEC
> (continuing)
> I think it needs a big idea . . . a hook . . .

Thanks a lot.

Even if you're not pitching your idea, the marshaling of
a pitch forces you to organize your ideas about a script . . .
and that's a good thing.

Readers Hate

Over the years, I've had many, many readers as my students and they have told me they're tired of reading scripts that open with:

> Dreams, because when the character wakes up, the reader/viewer inevitably feels ripped off after having invested themselves.

> Heroines who have important jobs because of hubby or father. Discounts them as people.

> Waking up and going to work. The reason readers don't like it when writers open scripts with their main character waking up, preparing themselves for the workday, is that, they, like myself, have read way too many scripts that open this way.

On the flip side, I'm convinced that in the hands of an inventive storyteller, a writer who twists the generic, who brings something new, something unique to waking up, it can be fresh and it can work.

Getting into the Business

I recommend the following, which is how I got to be a screenwriter.

I was fired from a job as an educational filmmaker as I had become the Fellini of educational films.

I cared only about the film, the shot. The client and the information were of secondary importance . . . and I was justifiably out of a job.

I was living with my girlfriend in a tiny cabin on the beach in Malibu . . . so I decided to write a feature spec script. My first.

I had my typewriter—that's a mechanical device that prints letters on a piece of paper—out on the beach and was working away on *Flagpole*, a story of two competing flagpole sitters in the 1930s.

In retrospect, a movie about two people who don't move off of small square platforms on top of tall poles is a little suspect, but, nonetheless, there I was, getting tan, writing, when a guy with a beard walks by.

MAN WITH BEARD
What are you doing?

LAZARUS
Writing a screenplay about flagpole sitters in the '30s.

MAN WITH BEARD
Really. You have an agent to represent it?

LAZARUS
Nope.

163

MAN WITH BEARD
How about I represent it?

And I had an agent.
That's how I recommend getting into the business.
I sold *Flagpole* to ABC, but they never made it.

Another route is more common.
Write.
Take screenwriting classes.
Join a writers group.
Write a lot.
When you have two good scripts, start sending them out.
Try and figure out what producer has the sensibilities that would sync up with your script.
Cast the ideal producer, then send it to them.
Send the script to anyone you know who has contacts in Hollywood.
If you don't know anyone like that, call the Writers Guild to get a list of producers or a list of agents.
Be resourceful.
Go up on on the Internet, look around.
Buy the screenwriting magazines, look for competitions.
Enter contests and competitions.
Write.

Write a lot.

Keep writing.

Pre-Writing

Sometimes I find myself sitting at the computer, not writing, staring dumbly ahead at my monitor, frozen in the headlights of my screenplay.

What's going on?

I'm not prepared to write.

Why?

Because the organizational tool—usually my expanded scene list—is inadequate and not serving me correctly.

What do I do?

I go back and expand my scene list and, more importantly, I pre-write the scene.

I leave the computer, move out into the sun with a yellow pad and start conceiving the scene, making notes, writing down dialogue ideas, running the scene down in my head so I know what I'm going to write.

Then, in a matter of seconds usually, I'm back at the computer and cooking again.

Shooting Yourself in the Foot

The joke to my close writer friends is that I am forever shooting myself in the foot in my screenplays.

After writing a good script, somewhere around page ninety my hero will inexplicably have sex with a Rottweiler. It's happened too many times to not think it's pathological.

Don't put things in your script that will offend unless they're part of the story and not gratuitous, or that's what you are sure you want to do.

The unconsidered, thoughtless, gay, racial stereotype, anti-Semitism, anything offensive, has no place in your screenplay.

Getting Out of Your Own Way to Write

The writer who does everything but write.
The classic.
I know them.
You know them.
You may be one.
The writer who has to do the laundry, or make the call, or weed the garden, or clean out their desk, or do more research, or pay the bills, or do just about any goddamn thing but write.
Well, it doesn't work that way.

A small story
My cinematographer, let's call him Bruce, asks me to see his relative, a cousin, a schoolteacher, who has moved

out to L.A. to be a screenwriter. Stand in line, buddy. I meet with him. A nice young man. He comes to my house on his bike. God love 'im. He gives me a script to read and pedals off.

Ten days later, he pedals back. I'd read his script. It was okay, generic, incorrectly formatted, the work of an amateur.

I ask him what film writing he had done in the last ten days.

He says he's written some observations in his journal.

I ask him what movies he had seen.

None.

Screenwriting?

No.

I tell him to go home. Go back to where he was from and continue being a schoolteacher.

The point?

He wanted it, but he was in the way of himself.

You really have to work hard to be a writer.

No one forces you to write. If you don't, you don't.

If you don't, do something else.

Don't Stop Momentum to Describe

A common mistake.

You have your script really cooking, the reader is whipping the pages by, swept away by your story, and you get to a new location and . . .

167

INT. SWEENEY MANSION - NIGHT

Arthur looks around. It's decadence personified.
There's food and drugs everywhere and then
there's the girls: blondes, nubile and barely
dressed, dancing and jiggling to TECHNO/HIP-
HOP, wild and untamed, brunettes, there must
be six of them, in white bikinis, lounging sensu-
ally on the leather settees, pouty and beautiful
in their innocence. All of this is the brainchild
of the Big Boys sitting at the end of the room in
their thronelike chairs, flutes of champagne in
their pudgy fingers, their fifty-dollar manicures
in no jeopardy of being scuffed.

Nice, but whatever story energy you had going is gone in
the morass of this ultimately meaningless description.
   When you're cookin' . . . don't stop it for anything but
the most minimal description . . . go with the energy, the
movement.

I Hate Montages

Because they break the screenplay form.
   They break the seduction of the reader we are building
so carefully.
   All of a sudden, in the middle of a screenplay comes
this:

MONTAGE
1. Arthur at a bar drinking.
2. Arthur walking the streets of L.A.
3. Arthur sleeping in a chair in living room.

You can accomplish the same exact thing and keep us in the script by not breaking form.

Write out the scenes in the same form as the rest of the screenplay and by doing that you won't break the flow of your screenplay.

For example:

INT. BAR - DAY

The afternoon sun shines through the venetian blinds onto the bar and into Arthur's bleary, bourbon-glazed eyes.

EXT. WILSHIRE BOULEVARD - DAY
Holding his hand over his eyes to cut the glare, Arthur leans up against the art deco building. He's tired. He's drunk. He's a writer.

INT. ARTHUR'S APARTMENT - NIGHT
The TV has a test pattern and HUMS. Two empty beer bottles on the table. Arthur is slumped over on the couch asleep. This doesn't look like a happy place.

So much richer. So much fuller . . . and without breaking the seduction.

Transitions

A vital part of the process of creating a script with real flow and readability.

I learned about how to make transitions in film writing in the editing room.

How scenes cut on film has a direct correlation to how they cut in a script.

The concept is: **scenes that look the same don't cut well, on the page, in your reader's minds, on the screen.**

You want to present to your reader very different images on the end of one scene and on the beginning of the next scene.

That means, if you end a scene this way:

Arthur makes it to the top of letter W, then sits
and catches his breath.

Which is a relatively wide shot, you don't want to go to another shot that looks the same, so you might:

INT. NEWS HELICOPTER - DAY

A blonde TRAFFIC REPORTER putting lipstick on freezes.

TRAFFIC REPORTER
Jesus, Fred, someone's on the friggin' W.

An example of scenes that don't cut together.

As Arthur, totally dispirited, walks out.

INT. ARTHUR'S APARTMENT - NIGHT

Arthur walks in.

They are two shots of Arthur that read much the same visually.
Here's how it should be done:

As Arthur, totally dispirited, walks out.

INT. ARTHUR'S APARTMENT - NIGHT

An empty wine bottle on the coffee table. In a
tee shirt and underwear, a weary Arthur comes
in from the crapper.

The rule is; **end a scene tight, open the next scene wide.**
If you **close wide, open tight.**
Before you finish your rough draft, read it only for transitions, check them out, see if they all work and help the flow.

Geography

One of the basics.

The reader should always know exactly where your characters are. This is particularly true in action scenes. Write, then rewrite your action carefully.

I dislike writing action scenes as much as any part of film writing. For me, it's mechanical, emotionless writing and holds little interest.

After the original conception, for me, they're boring to write. I write scenes like this carefully once, rewrite them carefully, then I skim them most of the read, only to read them real carefully again before I ship the damn thing out. This kind of writing should be simple and direct.

Metaphors and Similes

Don't work because they conjure up non-movie images.

> INT. HOLLYWOOD STUDIO - HALLWAY - DAY
> Arthur runs down the hall like a wounded hippo fighting its way out of a mud pit.

Suddenly, in the middle of a script about a Hollywood film writer, my mind is thrust into a muddy safari scene.

Sex and Violence

How much?

Most times, the erotic material I've written and directed has made mainstream producers and development people squeamish. I wrote an original, a spec screenplay, *Free Run*, for the producing team of Foster/Turman and Universal based on a pitch.

The pitch was: A man in his mid-thirties falls obsessively in love with a twelve-year-old girl.

It was about a man in search of innocence.

About fantasy versus reality.

It made everyone so nervous that, when I handed in the first draft, they were crazed.

The girl was too young.

We raised the age.

I warned them that innocence, these days, is real young. If we don't play that, it's not going to work.

Every draft I did, they insisted I make the girl older, from fourteen, to sixteen, to, finally, nineteen.

When Universal finally read it they said it didn't work.

No wonder, they were right.

On the other hand, nearly every erotic script I've ever written has been bought.

When I tried to come up with a strategy for becoming a feature director, I realized I didn't want to direct TV, which wasn't the kind of directing I was interested in doing . . . too corporate and formulaic. A story within a story: when working on a series, I became friendly with an actor who was hustling to direct an episode. When the studio finally gave it to him, he was really excited, went to work and came in totally prepared, shot lists, story boards, the whole shooting match. On the first day, the first scene, he went to the cinematographer to talk with him about how he saw the coverage. The cinematographer listened to him describe his shots, then smiled and said, "Let me show you how we do it." And that's what they did.

So, since I didn't want to direct TV, I knew I'd have to direct low-budget features.

Most of low-budget fare is crime, thriller, teen murder, horror, violence, all of it.

I don't like to see, read, shoot, anything with violence. I turn away from the screen, or hold up my hand when those images are on. I don't want that stuff in my consciousness. So, I went back to the old chestnut about "write what you know," and I applied it to directing and decided to focus on erotica. I'm now prepping to direct my fourth feature.

And I've found that world to be terribly conservative. Not knowing anything in terms of marketing feedback or market testing, the execs are forced to depend on subjective opinions . . . and subjective opinions in the area of sex are so . . . so . . . subjective, it can make you crazy.

The short of it is: **a little sex in a script goes a long way. Write it so your mother can read it.**

Don't make it terribly graphic.

Indicate what you want to appear on the screen and don't rub anyone's nose in it, so to speak.

The same goes for violence.

You don't have to write splatter and disgusting gore, though God knows, those films get made.

You're going to have a wide range of readers and you don't want to turn off potential buyers with too-graphic descriptions.

The unrelenting gore in the first twenty minutes of *Saving Private Ryan*, which everyone applauded as art, I thought was disgusting, no better than the countless straight-to-video slasher movies, just more expensively shot. I felt it was equally gratuitous and offensive and troubling. To think that an assault of violence like that is tolerated and applauded, and nudity and sexuality is legislated against is mind-blowing to me. I am clearly a minority voice.

Dialects

I occasionally run across a script that takes place in New Orleans and the writer, who knows the area intimately, writes most of the characters as Creoles and Cajuns, and it's like a meeting of the United Nations.

It's an impossibly difficult read.

It gets in the way.

At best, indicate a little of how your characters speak. Here's a simple way to deal with it:

Arthur wiped the nervousness off his palm and held out his hand to shake.

                    ARTHUR
        My name's Arthur.

DOLA, the Creole actress, smiles provocatively.

                    DOLA
                (Cajun accent)
        I love you, I just do.

Also, in a world obsessed with political correctness, someone may take offense at your writing like a Cajun or whatever. Like writing about sex, a little dialect writing goes a long way.

Exposition

Information the writer needs to communicate to the reader/viewer for the story to work.

The deal is, if you need to communicate the information you want to **hide exposition.**

Hide it in attitude, in a fight, in action. It's a little of the old sleight of hand, but it's not like we're doing brain surgery or something here.

An example of how you shouldn't do it:

EXT. STUDIO PARKING LOT - DAY

Arthur tries to keep up with Simon Sweeney as he walks to his Jaguar.

> ARTHUR
>
> Simon, we have a long history, you and me, back when you were an agent, and you sold my script, and handed it to one of your clients and they totally rewrote it, then you went to the studio as head of production and shitcanned the picture, you owe me.

Obviously not a "real conversation."
How you should do it:

EXT. STUDIO PARKING LOT - DAY

Arthur tries to keep up with Simon Sweeney as he walks to his Jaguar.

> ARTHUR
>
> Simon, we have a long history.

SIMON

Get away from me.

ARTHUR

You fuckin' owe me.

SIMON

I'm calling security.

DEVELOPMENT EXEC

You shot my picture down, you owe me.

Simon has his cell phone out.

SIMON

This is Simon Sweeney. I need security in
the executive parking lot.

When characters are telling other characters things they
know . . . watch out. Be very suspicious. Rewrite.

The thing about exposition is it **tells** the reader/viewer
the information. Take that out of the script and the reader/
viewer **learns** the information. I think the latter way involves the reader/viewer in a more interesting way. It asks
more of the reader/viewer but they end up getting more.

Shooting Yourself in the Foot, Part Two

I've seen way too many scripts with the flaming gay
queen, the extraordinary Black athlete, the stingy Jewish

businessman. I've read scripts where only one of the characters' religion is named, when racial or religious stereotypes have been inadvertently written into a script.

When I ask the writer why he labeled only the Jew's religion in the script, the writer never really knows.

The rule is be careful.

You don't really want to offend anyone.

Reviews

A real aid to film writing.

Reviewers are usually smart people analyzing what's wrong with movies. You can learn from others' mistakes.

Sometimes reviews are written by Hollywood sycophants who drool unnaturally over the product so they can make the quote ads. Those reviews are meaningless.

Reading well-written, thoughtful reviews makes you understand the issues involved in making scripts and films work.

Of course, you have to pick your reviews and reviewers. The local reviews of *Austin Powers* may just be as valuable, may teach you more, than Pauline Kael's review of *Parallax View*, though somehow I don't buy it.

Coverage

The reports readers give to their bosses.

While writing this book, the producer of a script of

mine, *In the Belly of the Beast,* up until now one of my most complimented scripts, sent me coverage from one of the cable channels.

"Lazarus employs a stylized, film noir approach which undercuts delivery of the full range of this potentially powerful, true story. His screenplay attempts only to take us into the mind of Jack Abbott and see, from his perspective, the brutal experience of prison. The result is a hollow, one-note exercise.

Whether intentionally or not, the script falls victim to the very same romanticizing of Abbott's life to which Mailer and others fell victim.

Lazarus even goes so far as to attempt to invoke sympathy for Abbott when he's arrested for killing Adan.

Lazarus has chosen a very subjective and insular approach which is not only intellectually disingenuous, but cinematically flawed as well. The script's first person perspective quickly grows tedious especially given the lack of story structure and cohesion. Exposition is almost nil.

The first third of the script has no momentum or direction but merely rehashes Abbott's prison experience. Upon his release, the scenes detailing Abbott's inability to adjust also lack direction and are cursory and uninvolving. They fail to build an inevitable momentum toward his murder of Adan.

. . . and it went on. . . .

They didn't mention how well it was typed.

The Hook

My dentist, let's call him Dr. Ted, asked to read one of
my scripts. I gave him the best one, i.e. the one I just
finished . . . they're always the best one, 'til the next
one . . . A couple of months later, while replacing a crown
to the tune of too much money, he told me he had read
the script . . . he was unsure how to voice the critique,
him being a dentist and all, so . . .

> DR. TED, curly hair, WHISTLING the theme to
> MARATHON MAN, packs my mouth with those
> white cotton dental mini-Tampax.

> ### DR. TED
> I really like it . . . but . . . I don't know, it
> needs a hook.

My dentist . . . incredible.
What he was talking about is the Big Idea, what grabs
us . . . the thing you hang the rest of the script on.

Clichés

> EXT. HOLLYWOOD HILLS - NIGHT
> Arthur's eyes were steely. He ran like a bat out
> of hell, past the dilapidated old red barn, past

the enclave of homeless people, over a white
picket fence, past the window of a farmhouse
where Arthur could see a pulchritudinous barefoot farmer's daughter, in a white peasant's
blouse and cut-off jeans, a girl as innocent as
fresh-drawn milk, waiting on her bed, legs
spread provocatively, her tongue wetting flame
red pouty lips . . .

You get the idea.

When I worked for prolific television producer Steve Cannell on *Hunter* and *Stingray*, he would not allow his writers to write characters saying clichés.

Why?

Because you're a creative type, right? You don't want
you or your characters to speak in clichés, do you?

The Sun to Yolk of Fried Egg Dissolve

If you do the above, you will rot in hell forever.

More Uncinematic Stuff

Computers — most of us writers spend so much time on the
computer, we forget how boring it is on film. It's boring.
Big time boring. A Little Goes A Long Way Department.

Action Sequences

The classic is:

The army takes the town.

Five words, and it could cost five million dollars with helicopters, troops, costumes, special effects bombing the town.

Don't cheat on action.

Write it the way you see it.

Don't be too detailed.

Always tell your action through the characters we care about.

Make sure you leave white space on the page to make it accessible.

Turning in Your Script

Always turn it in on time . . . not early.

You win nothing for turning your script in early. You only end up with a producer who thinks you haven't spent enough time on it.

Always look exhausted. Never have a suntan. It took everything out of you to write this masterpiece and you want the people who aren't paying you enough to know it.

Always register your script with the Writers Guild of America. There are registration offices at both the Writers Guild East and West. It's ten bucks for members, twenty for nonmembers. A smart thing to do. Why? Because if anyone ever steals your idea, you'll have a record of your work. Then you don't have to worry about it.

Turning Things on Their Ear

Never said enough.

Make it original.

If it feels familiar, it is . . . and change it.

An example: a gender bender . . . take a familiar male buddy action movie, cast it with women and you have *Thelma & Louise*.

The Best Friend

Heroes get mighty lonely alone.

No one to talk to, plan with, plot against.

The best friend is someone to talk to. . . .

Someone to care for when they die . . .

Someone to betray the hero . . .

Someone to stand on to get in a window.

You get the idea.

Characters Who Speak Out Loud When No One's Around

Kill them.

When you do write characters who speak out loud, usually to tell the audience something they won't otherwise have a chance to know, get up from the computer, walk outside, reach around and kick yourself in the butt, then walk back inside and rewrite it.

Coincidences

They're the worst.

Coincidences usually indicate lazy writing. You can't figure out something in the story . . . so, magically, coincidentally, your hero stumbles upon the 1939 cover of *Life* magazine which provides the clue he or she's been looking for. Spare me. Work harder.

What Should You be Writing?

A difficult question to answer. Many times, at the beginning of a semester, I'll have a student who has three script ideas and doesn't know which to write.

Usually I say, write the idea you have the most passion for.

And if You Don't Have an Idea?

Open yourself up . . . look at everything as a potential movie . . . read newspapers, browse weird links on the Internet . . . allow yourself head quiet time . . . get in touch with feelings or things you want to write about. Go to the library.

Once, when I was dry for an idea, I made a list of the top ten grossing movies of all time, took the trailer elements of each of them and tried to fashion a script. Luckily, a real idea came along and I could move my energies to that.

The Writer Who Doesn't Finish

Maybe you know a writer like this. A million ideas, started four or five screenplays, lots of energy, then the same thing happens: thirty, maybe fifty pages in, the writer loses energy.

Second thoughts creep in.

The script's in terrible trouble.

Lost, the writer abandons the script.

I'm not sure this is the book to deal with the issues involved. Fear of success. Fear of failure. Bad organization. I have no idea.

But, if you are such a writer, my suggestion is decide, from all your abandoned screenplays, the one you have the most faith in, the most passion for . . . and finish it.

No matter what.

Get to the end, write The End.

Then rewrite, get to the end, finish it.

Put it down and see how it feels.

Once you've finished a script, it will forever give you more confidence for the next one.

It's a lot more satisfying than quitting in the middle.

And you don't have to show it to anyone . . . but it's always part of it for me, to await the reactions . . . good and bad. Better good than bad, but sometimes, in the face of bad reactions, you have to stick to your guns and say, this is what you want your screenplay to be.

Other times listen to the notes.

If everyone says you're dead . . . you just might be dead.

Television

It used to be a dirty word. A film writer work in television? Please. It was considered a low-class medium. Low common denominator entertainment. Feature writers wouldn't be caught dead working in television.

My how things have changed. Everybody works in television these days. It's matured. So have we. Some of the most interesting long-form projects anywhere are being made for television. Sure, some of it's impossibly dumb, but there are some wonderful things as well.

Writing for a television series is fabulous fun. Fabulous money. Fabulous hard work.

I started my career in television writing by writing freelance episodes of two long-ago series, *Charlie's Angels* and *Columbo*. I remember the experience as incredibly painful . . . *Columbo* more than *Angels*.

The executive producer/writer, the Showrunner, the power on *Columbo*, was an egomaniacal TV veteran, let's call him Robert. I got the assignment because he was represented by the same agent I was, which is a very common way to get work. The better your representation, the more power they wield for you. I came in with a story, he liked it and I was off and writing. I did a whiz-bang job and sent in my first draft . . . then the fun began.

I did a notes meeting . . . this is where he tells me how I've screwed up and why he's so smart and why he's running the show and I'm just a lowlife freelancer.

This was my first experience with the dreaded EXEC-UTIVE PRODUCER PRIVILEGE. This is how it works: you say something . . . you're a jerk. He says something, often times the exact same thing . . . he's a genius. There's no logic, no right or wrong, no common sense. He's right. You're wrong. And they give you a lot of money.

My most distinct memory is sitting in front of Robert's desk while he dictated dialogue, dictated scenes, dictated exactly what he wanted. Then, I'd go home and write them. Having come from writing/producing/directing my own films and writing original screenplays, I hated being discounted the way I was . . . then they gave me a lot of money and I felt better.

The episodes of these two series came out well. Robert didn't go for credit, which was gracious of him, so I received sole credit on each.

That writing, and selling my first screenplay, *Flagpole* — the previously mentioned, outrageously uncinematic one — got me hired as a staff writer on the TV series *Knightrider*, the show about a talking car with David "Soon to be a *Baywatch* hunk" Hasselhoff.

Boy, was I out of my element. I was used to being alone

on the beach writing. *Knightrider* meant staff writing and story meetings at Universal City, the self-proclaimed "Entertainment Capitol of the World."

The story meetings worked this way. We'd all meet in the executive producer's office. There were five of us: the executive producer; the supervising producer, the writer who's in charge of the writing staff, a spindly, neurotic guy; two Story Editors, who are writers with titles, who make more money than me; and me, the new kid on the block. The purpose of these story meetings was to "break" stories. It's a free-for-all of ideas that get written down on a green or white board and the episode is constructed, beat by beat, out of everyone's ideas.

Not only had I never been to one of these story meetings, I'd never even heard of them.

The hard lesson I learned, too late, as I was fired after five weeks, was to the aggressor goes the spoils.

The supervising producer, let's call him Gary, would leap to his feet, elbow the other writers out of the way as if he were going up for the rebound, never letting anyone else talk, stepping on other writers' ideas, leaping in and finishing others' sentences.

I was appalled at this behavior, how ungentlemanly . . . until I realized he was the star, his ideas were ending up on the white board, and I was the quiet, polite and, ultimately, unemployed jerk.

Based on my huge success on *Knightrider*, my agents pitched me to Frank Lupo, the creator of *Hunter*, who was hiring staff at the Steven J. Cannell Company. Lupo asked me to come up with some ideas for episodes. I watched the show and came in to see him with a show about pornography and snuff movies. Lupo liked the ideas, asked me two questions about how I knew this dark material and hired me as story editor to work under legendary executive producer Roy Huggins, the man who created *The Fugitive* among other of television's landmark shows.

Roy taught me a lot. He's got a terrific story sense and I was his fair-haired boy for the first half season, until he perceived I had screwed up and then he treated me like crap.

I wrote a two-parter called "Rape and Revenge" which got me lots of acclaim, as well as an episode in which the star, let's call him Fred Dryer, the ex-football player, who acted like the defensive end he was, was called on to wear a pink wig, makeup, eye shadow, glitter and lipstick, kind of a punk rock glam queen on steroids. I loved it. Fred hated it. The photos of Fred in pink wig and makeup hit every newspaper and tabloid in town. He told the pro-·ducer that I'd never work in this town again.

It was terrific fun. I wrote five episodes, story edited and rewrote a bunch more. Making a big weekly salary, being paid for each individual script, being paid a small weekly program fee, then getting money, residuals, every time the show is repeated on the air. It's the veritable gravy train for writing, for doing something I love. A great deal.

My strategy on *Hunter* was to write as fast and as much as possible. The network only orders a certain number of scripts so there's a finite number of script assignments to be had. We had three staff writers: one a story editor, one a staff writer, one a story consultant. They all are virtually the same job, writing, breaking stories; they're just different pay scales based on experience and the title of your last job. The requirements for these jobs are ephemeral at best. You can get the job because you and the show-runner have the same agent. I got this job because the showrunner liked what goes on in my head.

The Steven J. Cannell Company was a great place to work. It's the closest I've come to working in a setup like the old studio system. Cannell had something like five shows on the air at the time and, like the old studios, had offices filled with writers. Because Steve is a writer himself, he treated us with more respect than we were used to.

The offices were large, air-conditioned, had nice ersatz antique furnishings (I think Cannell's family's in the furniture business, so he got a deal) and we each had our own secretary.

It was fun working and playing with all the writers. Whenever anyone was having a problem, there was always a writer around to help figure out the solution. Anytime I needed a joke, I'd go next door to Bill Nuss, once a stand-up comedian, then a network executive, now a writer/producer, and he'd give me one free of charge.

From *Hunter*, Steve Cannell moved me to a start-up show called *Stingray*, starring Nick Mancuso. It was something about a man of mystery who drove a Corvette and helped people. Steve took me, another story editor and the supervising producer, let's call him N., to meet Nick, to get a sense of who he was and what he wanted out of the character.

Nick was really nice and kept making the point about how centered and spiritual he was and how he was only eating macrobiotically and that was vital to the success of the series.

Later that season, I had to talk to Nick about script changes and went to his trailer, where he was wolfing down a Big Mac and fries with both hands.

The supervising producer, N., was a very different breed than Roy. N. was neurotic big time. A chain smoker, N. was a lot more insecure than Roy, and would keep things away from the other writers, not tell us what was going on, hog the meetings with Cannell. Not a good guy.

One-hour television scripts are forty-seven to fifty-six pages depending on the show, broken into, in most cases, a teaser, four acts and a tag. They're fun to write, they go quickly and the WGA minimum for writing one of these as of the year 2000 is $26,645, not including residuals that in some cases can add up to an equal amount of money or more. To this day I'm receiving checks from the much syndicated *Hunter*. *Stingray* was never syndicated because there weren't enough original episodes shot.

Shows have the potential of going into syndication after they've shot a hundred episodes.

When you're on staff, the story is usually broken in story meetings: the outline is put up on the white board and designed and analyzed by the staff. Then, the writer of the episode does a beat sheet, which is every major beat of the story, put down in the four-act television structure, sometimes with teaser openings and tag scenes. Different shows have different designs as to how detailed the beat sheet is. The beat sheet is then sent to the network, the owner, the powers that be. You receive notes on the beat sheet before beginning your writer's draft.

After handing in the writer's draft you get notes from the supervising producer, maybe the exec and the other writers, then you do those notes and you have your first draft, which goes to the network.

Once you get the network notes, depending on the show, the script is either taken away and polished by the supervising producer or the executive producer, or you get to do their notes.

After that, the director comes on and he gives his notes, though many times, in TV, the director really doesn't have input on the script other than production considerations.

He shoots what he's given. There are always production notes which reflect the actual locations and changes due to location and casting variables, then they shoot it.

You have to write real fast in television. At the outside they give you two weeks to write your writer's draft. Some shows give you a week.

When I was working on *War of the Worlds*, Paramount, the producing entity, threw out one of our scripts on a Wednesday. The show was scheduled to shoot on Friday. We had no reserve script. Big trouble. Another writer and I wrote a full, shootable script for the hour show in two days. We worked out the beats, split up the acts and took off, rewrote each other's work and they shot it. That's the fun and excitement of television.

When you begin a season, it's always preferable to have at least six scripts in the can and ready to go. The reason? Once you start production, the scripts start being shot and, before you look up, you've shot your reserve scripts and you're under the gun to keep producing good scripts and that pressure can make grown writers do drugs, drink, eat too much, or go crazy.

From *Stingray*, I went to *Starman*, a show based on the Jeff Bridges movie, starring the wonderful comic actor Robert Hayes.

That show was top-heavy as there were two executive producer/writers, two producer/writers, one supervising producer/writer, a story consultant/writer and me, the low man on the totem pole. Plus, we used freelancers. And the show still wasn't very good. Why? Because how long can you play an alien looking at something and saying . . .

ALIEN
    Toilet plunger?

I had a particularly difficult time on that show as it was a bit more sappy than what I'm used to writing, and I had a difficult time finding the voice of the show.

On the other shows I'd worked on, because I was writing so much, my voice, many times, became the voice of the show. But, on *Starman*, I don't think I ever got it.

The two executive producers, two nice guys named Jim and Jim, came in one day and fired me. They were all really nice people and they did the right thing. I ended up writing two scripts that were made and were pretty good. The show didn't last a second season.

I then went on *Jake and the Fatman* and that was pretty odd. I worked for the person I consider the ideal supervising producer, TV veteran Phil Saltzman.

A gentle man, experienced, secure, unaddicted, nonneurotic, Phil ran a really tight show, spending most of his creative time breaking stories with the writers . . . not in huge meetings with eight writers fighting to be heard. Phil's story meetings were civilized and thoughtful . . . and efficient . . . and we left work each day at six. . . . Good deal. He had a very small staff: himself, me and Frank, who read and critiqued scripts, but did very little writing, and we put out the show. Great fun.

Unfortunately, the show was not terribly good, which many times in television doesn't seem to be very important. From there, I made a move that made my agents unhappy. Rather than go to another network show where there's more money and prestige, I wrote for a syndicated show I previously mentioned called *War of the Worlds*, which, I'm proud to say, a newspaper in Arizona called "the worst show on television."

The show was truly bizarre. It was shot in Toronto on a minuscule budget with mostly Canadian crew and cast . . . which is problematic in some ways as it's not the best crew you can get, it's the best Canadian crew you can get.

My favorite story of what "Canadian crew" means is: we hired someone and one of her jobs was to check through the scripts for continuity errors.

After about five shows I asked her if she'd found any continuity problems on the show we were about to shoot. "Yes," she said. She'd found some. "And?" I said. Seems she hadn't figured out that as part of her job, she was supposed to give someone the results of her search. She had the lists neatly stacked on her desk.

I worked a full season on *War of the Worlds*, then Paramount cleaned house and brought in all new producers and writers and the show went off the air. I like to think if they had kept us, we'd've been number one.

One of the problems I encounter when writing for series is once I've written the show for a few months, I get bored and want to stretch a little. This is not encouraged at all. Once a TV show finds itself, gets its formula together and is getting ratings, networks and exec producers are loathe to change it. For me, it's boring writing the same thing week after week. Short attention span or something, so by the end of the first year, I'm always looking for something that sparks me.

War of the Worlds was a fabulously cheap show. I remember the executive producer lining up the actors on the set, having them stand in front of the camera, do their lines, move off, then he put the next actor in, they'd do their line and so on.

War of the Worlds was the show I had the most fun on because there were only three staff writers including one exec producer, and he was more interested in playing golf than writing, so the other writer and I worked real hard, made a lot of money and had more control on this show than any other I worked on. "Worst show on television," indeed.

After that I was hired and quickly fired from *Freddy's Nightmare*, the series, where I was supervising producer. I was responsible for creating the twenty-two-show season of one-hour stories. I had replaced a person I'd never met, let's call him Jeff, who had been retained as a consultant, and whose new job it was to critique the writing as it was generated. He was so vociferous about his dislike of the writing that he ultimately poisoned Warner Brothers TV, the producers, and they told the executive producer to tell me that I should be writing more like Jeff, the man they didn't want doing the job anymore. I told the exec that I couldn't write like Jeff, that I would be writing like Tom this season. He said I should go home. I said he'd have to fire me. And he did. And I got a big settlement and wrote *Stigmata*. So there.

Writing half-hour sitcoms is something I know nothing about other than:

1. Boy, do those writers make a lot of money.
2. Those shows have ten, sometimes fifteen writers on staff. What do they all do?
3. Most of the shows are unwatchably dumb and unfunny.
4. Word has it they work real hard, all of them, sitting in the room all night, think-

ing up lines, coming up with situations, jokes and character stuff. Sitcom writing, from everything I've heard, is real hard work. I don't get it.

Is writing for television different than writing for features?

I don't really think so. It's all film writing. I've always felt because of the way people watch TV, with the lights on, doing other things, eating, walking in and out of the room, talking to other people in the room, TV is a much more sound-oriented medium than movies. Less room for subtlety in dialogue. People are anchored in the story more with sound than pictures. I don't know how that fact translates into the writing except maybe subconsciously.

Freelance writing is tough going.

You have to have a lot of discipline, fortitude and good fortune. You have to show up every day. I have projects in different stages of development.

At the moment I write this, I'm finishing one script, have researched and am waiting to write another and I'm in presentation/concept stage on a third. I'm forever servicing my older scripts, re-Xeroxing them on fresh white paper, making sure the brads aren't rusty, updating addresses and area codes.

• • •

Freelance episodic is particularly tough.

Most of the staffs like to write their own episodes. This season, David Kelly writes each episode of three of his series!?!

If you're fortunate enough to get to go in and pitch a series, you go and pitch maybe three different story areas. Odds are, they're developing one like yours already, they flat out don't like another because their star said he'll never appear with midgets, and the third idea isn't bad. They give you some ideas how to make it more "their" show and tell you to work it up into a pitch or pages so they can submit it to the supervising producer.

Of course, you've got to be pitching a number of series to make a living, so it's a big deal hustle. Lots of driving, lots of pitching, lots of rejection. You get turned down many more times than not. That's one of the reasons they pay us so much when we are working. It kind of balances the universe.

Lots of TV writers and wannabe TV writers write spec scripts: an episode of *Ally McBeal* or *Law & Order*, to show how they write TV.

I've actually never written a spec of an existing show. I'd much prefer to show my original writing to a buyer, rather than my ability to ape another writer's style. I prefer showing another how I write characters, how I structure, how I solve creative problems, rather than how I can copy other writer's writing.

My view is the minority one here.

How do you get into the TV business?

If you find out, tell me.

Shows are staffed one of two ways . . . who the executive producer knows and who the executive producer's agents know. In either case you have to be connected . . . or have a hit. It's not easy.

Fooled Them Again

As of this writing, I've just been hired to come up with the characters and stories for a twenty-four-show season of half-hour shows for the Playboy Channel. I will write and direct half of the shows. What's wonderful about a gig like this is the amount of creative freedom they give me. They have to give me that as they sure don't give me enough money. I'm very excited about this and, if all goes well, the show should premiere about the same time this book comes out.

Addendum

As of this rewriting, all those people at *Playboy* who hired me and liked what I do have been fired. The new administration, never ones to like the fruits of the outgoing administration, have asked me to retool the show. Meaning? They have to piss on it to make it their own.

I'm here to serve.

MUCH MORE THAN A GLOSSARY

Actors — I love them. What they do is so difficult and the good ones work so hard, are so into it.

They've taught me so much about character development.

When I went in to rehearsals on the first feature I directed, called *Movies Kill*, which should have been called *Producers Kill*, because of the nutsiness of my producer; that aside, I had worked on the script for six or seven months and thought all the character development had been done.

Not according to the actors.

That's what makes them so great. They started asking me questions about the characters, wanting to develop them, get inside of them. It forced me to get back into the characters, go deeper and the film was much, much better for their probing.

Mark Pellegrino, one of my favorite underappreciated actors, who's appeared in all of my features in a starring role, is a fabulously thoughtful actor. He drives the crew crazy because he needs time to get into the character.

With the kind of schedules I've been shooting, every second counts.

I've had to convince the crew that just as they need tech time to set up the shots, the actor needs his time, too. They grumble at me. Actors have to put it out there, while we all get to hide behind the camera or the page.

When actors are good, they warm your heart.

When actors are bad, they're fingernails on a blackboard.

Agents — Swine. Let me tell you a story. A few years back, I had a golfing agent. We got together after he told me my career was in a shambles and he was the perfect agent to resurrect it. He had read three of my scripts and was effusive in his praise. He was touched, "tears came to his eyes," I was a "brilliant" writer. Of course, I went with him and settled back to reap the benefits of my upcoming career resuscitation.

After a few months—he had gotten me no work—I sent him a rough draft of my new script. He read it and told me that women didn't like it. I asked him how he arrived at that. Turns out he gave it to his secretary, who'd been in the business all of five minutes, she didn't like it, so "women didn't like it." That was that.

I rewrote it, tried to make it more woman friendly, then gave him the next draft to read. He thought it should be funnier. I said okay and rewrote it again.

When I finally gave him what I considered the first draft, he read it and called me.

He said it wasn't funny enough and suggested he bring in another writer to "punch it up."

I couldn't believe it.

My agent bringing in *another* writer on *my* original script?

Flabbergasted, I told him I'd call him right back.

I hung up, went to my computer, wrote him a letter terminating our relationship, faxed it to him within three minutes and never saw or spoke to him again.

He had a four handicap . . . I should've known.

On the other hand, I've had terrific agents. The best was Norman Kurland, founding partner of Broder, Kurland, Webb and Uffner, one of the top agencies in Hollywood. Norman always read my work and was supportive of my vision, unlike many of the agents of today, who believe they should be the one who decides what their writer/ clients should be writing.

Anyway, even though I was clearly one of his lesser clients, Norman never let me feel that, always took my call, read my work quickly, had cogent comments and worked his butt off for me. His greatest gift was making me feel as if I was not only his most important client, but his only client. Smart, nice man.

I told my present agent, when we were in the get-to-know-each-other phase, that I tried always to tell the truth. Her reaction? "Oh, my."

As a rule, I trust agents as far as I can throw them, and I have a bad back.

Air — An issue with my writing. Because I go for flow and speed of reading, there are times in my scripts when everything is going too fast . . . there's no air. Then I'll insert a scene that rests . . . an elongated transition or my main character contemplating something. I now have to consciously take a draft and examine where the storytelling needs to breathe between beats.

Beat Sheet — A story organizing tool. A list of scenes broken down by acts outlining the basic story dynamics and movement of the characters.

Development — When *Stigmata*, a film I wrote, became the number one movie in the country the week it was released, my agents sent me on what I affectionately referred to as the TOM LAZARUS "STIGMATA" TOUR, 1999.

I met with development people from ten production companies and two studios. Development people are writer-friendly people and therefore I love them. They actually talk about writing, stories, scripts; it's amazing. They're uniformly young. It's a starting point to becoming producers, I guess. Some of them are writers.

The meetings are pretty much the same. We talk. They tell me about their company or studio, what pictures they have in the hopper, what they're looking for.

Then, I tell them what I'm working on, usually the script I'm writing, the one I've just finished and the one I'm researching. Because these are meet-and-greet get-togethers, it's not an official pitch, there's no performance anxiety. We're just talking. But, they get to see how I think and the kind of projects I'm working on.

One of my poignant memories of the "STIGMATA TOUR" was walking into a producer's office on the Fox lot and the receptionist was the development guy. I felt for him as he answered the phones, then we had our meeting. A real nice guy. We had lunch. We talked. It was fun. I like development people.

Dumbing Down Scripts — I had a student who, in a thriller screenplay, kept repeating important information every fifteen pages or so. When I called him on it, he explained that readers in the industry were so dumb he felt it was a necessity. I implored him to write his script smart. Don't underestimate the reader/viewer.

Eggs on Eggs — I was working on *Starman*, the TV series, when I had the great pleasure of working with the late Leon Tokatyan, a flamboyant, eccentric, extremely talented writer, who created the series *Lou Grant*. He had an expression, "eggs on eggs." He used that whenever a writer was hitting something too hard, being repetitive or just going too far. It's stuck with me and is a terrific way to check yourself and keep in balance.

The First Page — Write it and rewrite it. Make it not too dense. Make it accessible. Make it grab the reader so they have to turn the page. Make them excited about the world you're creating.

A First Look — When I went out with my script *Crazy in Love*, I gave the first look—a small, exclusive window where he and he alone had the script—to an old friend, let's call him S., who had become the hottest comedy producer in town. My hope was we'd get to work together and I'd make a lot of money. He passed.

Flashbacks — I'm not a big fan because, instead of moving a story forward, flashbacks send it backwards.

Flow — The ease of reading. Nothing jars. It's all a single piece. A smooth ribbon that never pops you out of the story. I've mentioned many of the techniques that contribute to a smooth flow: transitions, logic of scene description, accessibly designed pages, comfortable language. Important to remember.

Harry from Miami — The original Harry optioned one of my first scripts, *Watershed*, another story of sex and

Hollywood. A hustler from Miami with a nine-inch cigar, Harry came to Los Angeles, had a suite at the Beverly Hills Hotel, a one-sheet showing the campaign, and a business prospectus two inches thick. He hadn't a clue how to be a producer or how to get a film launched. I never heard from him again.

I've had a hundred, a thousand, meetings with these Harrys from Miami.

They all believe it's going to happen.

They all believe this is the big one.

I will continue to go to these meetings.

I, too, believe the next one is going to be the big one.

Hit — *Stigmata* has been my only bona fide hit. As I've said, it was the number one picture in the country the week it was released. At the time of this writing it has grossed fifty million dollars domestic and is projected to be a moneymaker for MGM, the releasing company. The domestic gross is considered to be twenty percent of the worldwide income on the film, all in. The film cost thirty-two million. After writing for twenty-some odd years, I finally have a hit. People say congratulations. People call on the phone. Reporters ask for interviews. I'm asked to speak at colleges and universities. It's terrific.

It has changed how people within the industry perceive me. Since the picture opened and did very well, I've been asked to be part of a project because, in the first case, a company was preparing a pitch with a writer for a sci-fi slot on Showtime, and they felt since Showtime is a notorious "star fucker," an endearing term for a company that likes to deal with the hot and successful, I, off the success of *Stigmata*, would be perfect.

In the second case, they asked me to develop a series they wanted to pitch to TNT, also a notorious "star fucker." A hit has given me more credibility, more people are interested in what I want to write and are interested in having me write something they need. It's wonderful. Without a hit, you can survive as I did for many years; with a hit you can hopefully do more than survive.

As I rewrite these pages some three months after *Stigmata* was a hit, people still remember, but there have been many more flavors of the week since then. My obituary will inevitably mention *Stigmata*. It's been fabulous even before MGM bought it. *Stigmata* was optioned three separate times. Each time I did a rewrite, plus I rewrote it a number of times for myself over the eight-year journey from idea to number one. Upon its video release, *Stigmata* was in the top five for both rental and sales.

Hollywood Question — While teaching up at University of California, Santa Barbara, one of my tenured colleagues approached me after class.

Could I answer a Hollywood question? Absolutely. I thought, smart, an academic asking a question of a veteran of the writing wars. He asked, "Is Wilshire Boulevard north or south of Santa Monica Boulevard?"

House Number — A term I learned on staff on a TV show. It's when another writer gives you an example of the kind of scene they're talking about, but it's not precisely what they mean. For example:

INT. SWEENEY'S OFFICE - DAY

In the middle of a creative roll, Arthur paces.

                         ARTHUR
          The house number is she walks in, stabs
          him in the chest, takes the attache case
          with a million dollars and flies to Toledo.

The Joke — I once had a student who wrote a script where the joke of the movie was you rubbed on some magic ointment and the rubbee sprouted wings. Another student wrote a script where the joke was stepping into a particular pair of shoes sent you back in time. When you have a script with a joke, you have to play it soon, play it often, and evolve it, so the joke doesn't just repeat. You must play the joke.

Laying Pipe — Putting something in your script early that pays off later. Setting up.

Mind Snaps, Memories, Memory Flashes — Boy, I'm getting tired of these. Every time a character thinks of something or remembers something, we flash back and see it. Do we really have to? Every time?

Missed Opportunities — Story opportunities, the potential of something in your script that remains unrealized. Characters, situations, wrinkles, options, choices are areas for missed opportunities.

No News Is No News — One of the most valuable things you can learn in this book. Here's the scene. You finished your script . . . it is by far the best thing you've ever written. You send it to your agent. She says she's going to read it over the weekend.

You hope that Sunday she'll call and say "I'm not finished with the read, but I just had to call you and tell you how incredible I think the script is."

But that call doesn't come.

Monday morning. You wait for the call to come around ten.

No call. All day no call.

Tuesday nothing.

She probably read it and hated it.

She's stuck it in an envelope and has sent it back.

The script never arrives.

A week later your agent finally calls to say everybody in the office read it and they love it.

The lesson?

No news is no news.

You know nothing, that doesn't necessarily mean that bad things are happening.

A difficult lesson to learn.

Notes — Reactions to a script, given to the writer, to improve the script. "Make it better" is not such a good note. "The second act sags because your action isn't rising" is a better note.

On the Nose — When your characters say exactly what they mean, when things go exactly as planned, when things are exactly what they appear . . . they are on the nose. An uninteresting choice. Not a good thing.

Parentheticals — Use them to explain dialogue that wouldn't be otherwise understood.

For example, this is wrong.

EXT. STUDIO PARKING LOT - DAY

Arthur has Simon Sweeney pressed up against a
Lincoln Town Car.
                    ARTHUR
          (pinning Simon's arms back)
You've got to do something to save me, for
chrissakes, it's all closing in on me.

Putting scene description in parentheticals is the common mistake.

Too many writers use parentheticals as writing crutches.

Use them only when you need to.

Here's a correct usage of parentheticals:

EXT. STUDIO PARKING LOT - DAY

Sweeney gets in Arthur's face.

> SWEENEY
> You're a basket case, Arthur, you've hit bottom.

> ARTHUR
> (totally unconvincing)
> Are you kidding, life is good.

Without the information in the parenthetical, the true meaning of the line would be unclear.

Percentage of Gross — I was a guest lecturer at the University of Miami and taking questions from screenwriting students. One asked me if I got a percentage of the gross on my deals. I barked at him that he should care less about the deals and more about writing, particularly while still in film school.

I'm always afraid that screenwriting students pick up

Variety, see millions of dollars being thrown at writers and think that's standard operating procedure out here.

A piece of advice; don't worry about the deal, there are people who can do that, lawyers, agents, accountants. Worry about the words. The words come first.

Petting the Puppy — Giving your main character something to do that's totally endearing and instantly gets the reader/viewer on their side. I've read scripts where the writer has put a petting the puppy scene in, literally. It's best to hide your blatant appeal for being liked as best you can. Here are two examples. In the Dustin Hoffman/Morgan Freeman movie called *Virus*, I believe, in the early going Hoffman has two big playful dogs he was petting. Early on in *Rocky*, Sylvester Stallone is characterized as a lovable guy because he pets a fabulously ugly dog. So easy.

Pitching — I know I deal with this earlier on, but I can't resist this story. I was pitching *Sacred Acts*, a TV show Davis Entertainment brought me in to work on.

I was pitching with Teddy Zee, president of Davis Entertainment and a terrifically bright, aggressive, stubborn creative executive. It was a show about a novice Catholic nun working for the Vatican's Congress of Sacred Acts. Halfway during the pitch, the head of series for TNT, a nice woman named Barbara Wall, asked Teddy if this was going to be a Catholic show. Teddy Zee said "Absolutely not. It's not a Catholic show at all."

TNT ultimately passed and we pitched it to Showtime
. . . and they loved the pitch. Teddy and I worked on the
leave behind for Showtime for a week when I got a flash
. . . the main character, the novice nun's issue was going
to be dealing with the "warm streak of sensuality that
coursed through her body." It explained everything: why
she was a nun, what kept her and another character together. It was terrifically exciting after working for literally
months on something, to finally see it clearly. After that
moment, I had pitch perfect on the pages and Teddy Zee
knew it. He gave me my first thank you. It was great.

Polishing — The final stages of rewriting. The last fi-
nesses that make your script perfect.
   The analogy to sculpting works here. The sculptor polishes the marble sculpture over and over again to make
it perfect. The same thing we do with scripts.

Readers — They do coverage, meaning they read a
script for a producer, a director, a studio, then synopsize
it and grade it according to the plot, the action, the characters, the dialogue, then make their recommendation
whether the producer should get involved. If they pan it,
more than likely the person they're working for won't even
read it. The irony of course is that many times readers are
rank amateurs.
   Once, one of my students, a reader for a producer, was
given one of my scripts to do coverage on.

I think she passed on the script.

I think she got an F in my class.

Reading Screenplays — My students tell me this is a really good thing to do, to see how other writers have solved problems, to compare the movies they've seen with how the writer wrote it. I've never done this. No real reason. Just too busy writing, I guess. More and more screenplays are being published. Give it a try. See if it helps.

Research — The reason a lot of writers are writers. You get to learn about tons of things.

I've mentioned a number of scripts so far. For them I've done research on: hearing dogs, U.S. currency, manic depression, psychopathology, man/beasts, mountain climbing, Frank Lloyd Wright, Orson Welles, CNN, flagpole sitting, extraterrestrials. I've spoken to a sexually harassed woman cop, a Mormon superstar (Marie Osmond — yes, I was one of the writers on their TV movie biopic), an Alaskan wilderness airplane pilot, a paraplegic-rights lawyer, cops who've been blown up by the Hell's Angels, deaf teachers, Franciscan priests, a wheelchair racer, Santa Monica detectives, L.A. Parole office psychiatrists, FBI agents, and a child psychiatrist.

Scenery Chewing — A negative theater term for an actor who is taking more than center stage, he's taking all of the stage and chewing the scenery as well. A tour de force performance that's over the top. Usually happens when there's a weak director or the actor is sleeping with the person financing the show.

Schmoozing — The small inconsequential talk before a meeting. Who's doing what to whom, who's out of a job, where'd they get their Mercedes detailed or the latest sex or studio embezzlement scandal. It's the first five minutes of a meeting where everyone pretends to be nice people. Early in my career I would cut the schmoozing time short and get right to the business. Wrong.

Executives want to do that human thing and it's smart to do it and be graceful about it. It's how you show people that besides being a good writer you are fun, interesting and a nonthreatening person to be around, not the monster you appear to be.

Showrunner — I went with my wife to visit an old actress pal of hers and her husband, a creator and showrunner of a sitcom that lasted nine years on network. Let's call him Randall. The showrunner is the person who is the final word on the show, the one with perfect pitch, the one who knows everything. A great job to have . . . tough to work for.

They're God and you're not.

We met at the house they were building. Randall told

us this is one of six properties on the coast of California that's over two and a half acres. That they bought this property two years ago. The property two estates away sold for fourteen million dollars.

There was a brand-new house on the property when Randall and his wife bought it, but it didn't work for them and they tore it down and are building an 18,000-square-foot house on the site.

He's been offered a million dollars profit on the property but he's not going to sell because he doesn't need the money. He said "he doesn't need the money" at least four times in the two long hours we spent with him.

He drives a brand-new bright red Ferrari.

He has a house in the mountains, a Hummer truck, a classic 1934 Desoto Airflow, and a new Mercedes. All this on nine years of a sitcom.

He hasn't worked in eight years, because he doesn't need the money.

I asked him if he writes. He said no one was paying him, why should he write.

He hates this business, hates the people in it, hates the product.

"He doesn't need the money."

Set Piece — A big physical, one-location, multipage scene. One of the highlights of your script. Hopefully a reason to make the movie.

221

Slug Line — The beginning of any scene in your script.

> The line which starts with **EXT.** or **INT.** followed by **THE LOCATION,** then **DAY** or **NIGHT.**

Spec — A screenplay you write on speculation, for no money, for no one. You're speculating that someday someone will come and pay you lots and lots of money for it.

Spine — The anchor your script is hung on. The A story, the heart of your piece. I find this one of the things I most refer to when critiquing scripts. "Is that scene on the spine of the movie?" *Very, very important to have a strong spine.* It is usually your log line. It involves your main character.

Spitballing — A heinous practice. Usually proffered by producers, when they enter the creative process, and usually off the top of their heads; with maybe five seconds of thought, they come out with ideas for the script you've been honing for three years.
"Let's make the guy a girl."
"Maybe the dog talks."
"Maybe instead of being lovers, he kills her."
"What if he's a college professor *and* a garbage man."
Whenever a meeting descends to spitballing, I become

very reticent and announce I love talking about story in meetings like this, but I've learned not to make binding decisions . . . that stepping back is a necessary part of the process. Most of the time, no one listens . . .'cause I'm only the writer. Sound bitter?

You bet.

I've seen too many scripts destroyed in "constructive" spitball meetings like that.

Short-Term Memory Loss — A very handy tool for re-writing. I found this out somewhat by accident. Due to herbal indiscretions earlier in my life, I have the short-term memory of a tomato.

That means, when I pick up a script I'm writing to read it . . . I don't remember large parts of it. Most of it, as a matter of fact. You've heard of the expression of "getting too close" to your work. With short-term memory loss, that is not a problem.

Short-Term Versus Long-Term Scene Solving — I do private consulting on scripts, and one of the interesting scripts had an interesting problem. The writer looked at each scene as a creative problem and solved it. He didn't take into consideration the overall creative solution of the script. Though each scene was solved, it wasn't solved in relation to the other scenes, creating a mess of a screen-play. Each scene, individually, was well written and interestingly conceived, but the overall was terrible. When he got what I was saying, he rewrote and saved the script, which turned out to be pretty good.

Standards and Practices — The TV Police. They read the scripts, look at the episodes to see if those nasty writers snuck any dirty, tasteless and offensive things into the shows. They're prudish, arbitrary and definitely a necessity.

My favorite story: I was writing *Hunter* and I opened the scene with a character on the phone . . .

CHARACTER
(into phone)
And the one in the middle's Willie
Nelson . . .

And the scene continues never referencing the above line. Well, it turns out that's the punch line to a dirty joke . . . and Standards and Practices had never heard it so it went through. It was a fleeting amusement when I wrote it, then never thought about it again. About a year later, I get a call from my father . . . a friend of his was watching TV in Florida, saw my credit, watched the show, heard the line, knew the joke and went crazy. The power of the medium.

Tipping — The practice of telling the reader/viewer what you're going to do, then doing it. How boring is that? An example:

INT. BAR - NIGHT

Arthur turns to the bartender.

                    ARTHUR
          I'm going to call Simon on the phone and
          give him a piece of my mind.

INT. ARTHUR'S APARTMENT - NIGHT

Arthur dials the phone.

                    SIMON
                (over the phone)
          Hello.

                    ARTHUR
          Simon, it's Arthur Pratt.

                    SIMON
          How'd you get this number?

                    ARTHUR
          I hate you.

I think it's infinitely more interesting to lose the first piece of dialogue so we open the scene with Arthur dialing and we don't know who he's calling.

Titles — Important. Something I search for on each project. I always write down titles, look for them in the writing. It's better than not to have a memorable title. When I worked at Universal, they were forever sending around memos asking for new titles on their upcoming releases. Each time they asked, for four years, I put the title *Make Me a Malted*. Never once did they name a movie that.

Tracking — As far as I know, a new phenomenon. The development people in Hollywood track writers and scripts. I found this out when my agent started getting calls from development people and producers the week before my script, *Crazy in Love*, was finished and ready to be sent out. It was great . . . to have people interested in my next script . . . it was a first and it felt great. Everyone passed.

Trademark Look — While working on a TV show, a writer came in to pitch me a story. He was a nice young man, wearing a shirt, sweater, slacks and loafers, without socks. Being the wiseass I am and trying to schmooze, I mentioned to him that he had forgotten his socks. He advised me that was his "trademark." Got me to thinking . . .

what's my trademark? Gut hanging over belt? Spaghetti sauce stain on my shirt? Nose hair? Write me before you choose your trademark; I'll let you know if anyone out here is using it.

Transcending Who You Are — I was writing a movie of the week for CBS and the main character was under a great deal of stress and I wrote that he fell asleep, just like me. The producer, a nice man named Phil Mandelker, was very gentle as he questioned me about it. I confidently explained the character was under stress, thus he sleeps, just like me. "Oh?" Phil said. He thought I should rethink it a little, that maybe the hero could do something more overt, acting out his stress. Of course, he was totally right. Since then, I've noticed that many times other writers write characters that approximate themselves. No big surprise, but a real trap. Make sure not all your characters do things the way you do. Mix it up. Use other people's behavior, not just yours, as a model for your character's behavior.

Wardrobe — How to dress as a writer? This is one of the biggies. I try and dress Rich Casual. Not too sloppy so you rub in their faces that you are your own boss. Not too dressy or you'll look like one of their parents. For you older people, try not to dress like your grandfather.

Screenwriting is a young person's game and you should at least attempt to look contemporary. On the *Stigmata* tour, I once wore a tee shirt, a good one, to a meeting and it worked. Never mind.

A Writer's Day — This is my schedule these days . . . my favorite schedule. Fight out of bed at 5:30 A.M. so I can get to the University of Southern California's swimming pool at 6:00 A.M. Swim for forty minutes, then return home and start writing by 7:15 A.M. That's the best time. My mind's clear, there are none of the day's distractions. Pure time. Then calls come in and it gets harder. That early time is when I do my most creative work of the day. Original writing is best then. Later in the day, I'll do rewriting, read student work, write letters, do business. I eat lunch early, before the crowds, then come back home if I have gone out, and do creative writing. I've got a second wind writing until around five or so . . . then I fade and answer e-mail, have an early dinner, then cool out at night and get to bed early. Makes me happy.

Writers Guild of America — I'm a card-carrying member. They track down residuals, have established fair labor practices and salary minimums. A good source for research, scripts if you're writing a spec for TV and it's open to everyone.

They have a reading library with scripts, books and videos. They have a great health plan and pension fund. A good thing. Not without problems, but what isn't.

Writing Around Scenes — This is a sneaky one. We all do it. When it's a real tough scene, lots of emotion, lots of conflict, something that is important, something that is difficult, we avoid it and don't write it. It happens off screen. Watch yourself. Show rather than tell.

Writing Groups — Groups of writers who meet, read each others' work, support and help each other. A terrific thing. Some of my classes have met years after we first got together. Join one. It helps . . . and makes you feel less alone.

Wrinkles — Twists and turns. Complications, surprises.

Writing Partners — Ah, writing partners. I've tried collaborating a number of times . . . all pretty much unsuccessfully.

One time, I was writing a script with a writer friend in New York. Let's call him Ed.

Ed and I spitballed on a story.

Being hotshots and smart guys, we didn't need an outline or a scene list. We were going to wing it, go with the flow.

Because of the three thousand miles between us, we decided to take turns writing.

He created characters. . . .

I created characters. . . .

We started alternately writing scenes.

By about page ten, my characters killed his characters.

We stopped writing.

My fault . . . I guess I'm a competitive writer.

Some people like writing with partners, someone to talk to, someone to bounce things off of, to commiserate with.

Me, I kill my collaborator's characters.

I write alone.

THE FINAL SECRET

EXT. HOLLYWOOD HILLS - NIGHT

News helicopters fill the air above the Hollywood sign. Moving through the low scrub brush,
black-outfitted SWAT thugs creep toward the
brightly illuminated letters. A news camera crew
and a REPORTER, whose stockings are shred-
ded by the overgrowth, holds a microphone into
the air.

                    REPORTER
Why are you doing this?

                    SWAT VOICE
Get down! Drop!

Sitting up on the giant W is Arthur, drunk, shirt
unbuttoned, waving a Cuervo Gold bottle
around in the air.

ARTHUR

Fade in: Exterior Hollywood Hills Night.
The army takes the town.

Arthur salutes the SWAT unit with his bottle.

LEAD SWAT
(through PA)

Come on down and there won't be any
trouble.

Arthur looks down . . .
. . . there are automatic rifles trained on him.

ARTHUR

Slow fade to black.

And carefully, Arthur climbs down off the W
and back to earth, where he's surrounded by
SWAT and taken into custody. The reporter
thrusts her microphone toward Arthur.

REPORTER

What's the secret? The final
secret?

Arthur smiles.

ARTHUR
The final secret is "keep writing."

FADE OUT:

The End.

END TITLES

I've just finished rewriting these pages for the last time
... it made me look back ... not only on the book, but
on what the hell I've been doing these last twenty-five
years as a film writer in Hollywood.

What was it all about? The endless meetings about projects that never went anywhere, those fifty or so screenplays, the thousands of different scenes, of different
characters, different twists and turns, all of it.

It was about the work, about writing, about creating ...
that's the spine ... whatever happened to the work, to my
film writing, was out of my control ... the writing, the
process of being a writer is what it was all about.

I guess that's why I'm happy.

—TLL

www.tomlazarus.com